Ana al-Haqq: Consciousness, Self, and the Quran, A SCIENTIFIC INTERPRETATION OF MANSOOR AL HALLAJ

Harsa khan

Published by Harsa khan, 2025.

ANA AL-HAQQ: CONSCIOUSNESS, SELF, AND THE QURAN, A SCIENTIFIC INTERPRETATION OF MANSOOR AL HALLAJ

First edition. May 24, 2025.

ISBN: 978-9334313093

Written by Harsa khan.

To the seekers of truth,

who dare to question,

who suffer for clarity,

and who strive to merge with the eternal essence

— beyond fear, beyond form, beyond name.

And to Mansoor Al-Hallaj,

whose cry of "Ana al-Haqq" echoes through minds

still bound by time and ego.

"And in yourselves, do you not see?"

— The Quran, Surah Adh-Dhariyat (51:21)

"Kill me, O my trustworthy friends,

For in my death is my life."

— Mansoor Al-Hallaj

Author's Preface

This book is the culmination of years of deep reflection, study, and an earnest quest to reconcile timeless spiritual truths with contemporary scientific understanding. *Ana al-Haqq: Consciousness, Self, and the Quran* is not merely an exploration of mystical philosophy or neuroscience—it is an attempt to rediscover what Mansoor Al-Hallaj truly meant when he uttered those controversial yet profound words, "Ana al-Haqq."

In an age where religious narratives are often stripped of their metaphysical essence or exploited for power, this work strives to restore depth, clarity, and intellectual honesty to the conversation. The story of Hallaj is not a relic of medieval mysticism—it is a mirror held up to our collective soul, questioning whether we have the courage to perceive the Divine not as an external idol, but as a universal consciousness in which we all participate.

This book does not preach religion. It does not ask for belief, but for observation and reasoning. Every assertion is made with a commitment to logic, psychological realism, and scientific support, without reliance on dogma, superstition, or mystical theatrics. My purpose is not to provoke, but to awaken—a faculty that resides in every thinking human being: awareness.

May this work inspire readers to look beyond inherited ideas and toward inner realization; to question not with rebellion, but with reverence; and to encounter the Qur'an and the self with new eyes—not bound by history, but illumined by insight.

— **Harsa Khan**

Index:

Chapter 1: Who Was Mansoor Al-Hallaj?

"And do not conceal the truth while you know it."
(Qur'an 2:42)

Introduction: The Necessity of Reclaiming Hallaj

Few figures in Islamic history have sparked as much controversy and fascination as Abu al-Mughith Al-Husayn ibn Mansur Al-Hallaj. To many, he is remembered as a mystic or martyr. To others, he was a heretic who challenged orthodoxy. But to those willing to peel back the layers of sectarian narrative, Hallaj represents something much deeper: a human being who reached a heightened level of consciousness — one that his contemporaries neither understood nor tolerated.

The modern world, equipped with advancements in neuroscience, psychology, and quantum thought, now offers us tools to interpret Hallaj not as a miracle worker or Sufi mystic, but as a **high-consciousness individual**. His famous declaration, *Ana al-Haqq* — "I am the Truth" — is not a claim to divinity, but a cognitive realization that demands scientific attention. This chapter initiates our journey to explore Hallaj from this radically grounded perspective.

The Man Behind the Name

Born around 858 CE in present-day Iran, Mansoor Al-Hallaj grew up in a society dominated by early Abbasid political theology and religious orthodoxy. His early exposure to the Qur'an and Islamic disciplines shaped his intellectual and spiritual development. However, unlike most religious scholars of his time, Hallaj was not content with passive acceptance of doctrines. He questioned, he sought, and most importantly — he **experienced**.

Historical records describe him as eloquent, intelligent, and fiercely committed to what he perceived as divine truth. He traveled extensively — from India to Mecca — absorbing diverse thoughts and philosophies. These travels played a critical role in expanding his consciousness beyond the narrow interpretations of institutional religion.

The Sociopolitical Landscape of His Era

Understanding Hallaj's execution requires understanding the world he lived in. The Abbasid Caliphate, though advanced in scholarship, was also deeply entwined with religious institutions that served the political elite. Anyone who questioned their interpretations of the Qur'an was seen not only as a theological threat, but also as a political one.

Hallaj's insistence on individual spiritual awakening, direct access to divine truth, and public preaching outside of institutional control made him dangerous. His thoughts threatened the monopoly of scholars (ulama) who interpreted the Qur'an not as a guide to consciousness and justice, but as a tool of control and sectarianism.

Ana al-Haqq: Misunderstood or Misused?

The statement *Ana al-Haqq* is the axis upon which Hallaj's entire legacy spins. Orthodox scholars of the time interpreted it as blasphemy — a man claiming to be God. But what if this interpretation is deeply flawed?

Let us examine this through **Qur'anic context and cognitive science.**

"Al-Haqq", meaning "The Truth," is one of the names of Allah. But the Qur'an also states:

> *"We will show them Our signs in the horizons and within themselves until it becomes clear to them that it is the Truth (al-Haqq)."*
>
> (Qur'an 41:53)

The verse clearly affirms that **al-Haqq resides both in the external world and within human consciousness**. The truth is not only "God out there," but "Truth within the self." When Hallaj declared *Ana al-Haqq*, it could be interpreted as a cognitive realization — an alignment between the self and the universal truth, as perceived by a highly evolved brain-state.

Neuroscience and the Levels of Consciousness

Recent neuroscience identifies various states of consciousness: from lower delta waves in sleep to higher gamma frequencies linked to self-awareness, unity perception, and insight. Mystical experiences, or what is termed in psychology as **"non-dual awareness"**, often arise in heightened gamma wave states, especially in the parietal and prefrontal cortex.

Studies on monks, meditators, and advanced cognitive states show that individuals can experience a collapse of the ego-self and feel **merged with a universal truth or presence**. But they are not delusional. Their brains function in highly coherent, integrated, and elevated neural synchrony.

It is highly likely that Hallaj's *Ana al-Haqq* experience was a **neurocognitive state of unified consciousness**, not a metaphysical claim of being God. He did not say, *Ana Allah* ("I am God"), but *Ana al-Haqq* — "I am the Truth." This is closer to saying "I have become one with truth" rather than "I am the creator."

The Psychology of Persecution

Why would a truth-based realization face such deadly opposition? Psychology offers an answer: **Ego-based consciousness** (which dominates most minds) fears the dissolution of its boundaries. When a higher mind speaks from the state of ego-transcendence, the lower mind perceives it as arrogance or heresy.

This was the case with Hallaj. He threatened the status quo not by claiming divinity, but by undermining the artificial walls built between human consciousness and divine truth. He dared to say that divine truth is accessible — that the human brain, purified of ego and societal conditioning, can experience al-Haqq directly. This was an unforgivable act in a society obsessed with control and hierarchy.

The Qur'anic Alignment of Hallaj's Thought

Far from contradicting the Qur'an, Hallaj's perspective aligns with it at a deep cognitive level. Consider:

> *"And He (Allah) breathed into him from His spirit..."*
> (Qur'an 32:9)

This suggests that every human being carries a fragment or reflection of divine consciousness. The Qur'an repeatedly urges reflection (*tafakkur*), understanding (*aql*), and inner purification (*tazkiyah*) — all of which relate to elevating the self to perceive truth directly.

Hallaj's teachings echo this. He did not invent a new religion. He invited people to **purify the ego**, to stop worshiping form, and to access **divine truth through inner awakening** — a message deeply Qur'anic in nature, though dangerous to religious institutions.

Execution: Silencing the Brain, Not the Soul

Hallaj was eventually imprisoned, tortured, and publicly executed in 922 CE in Baghdad. His body was destroyed, but his words could not be. His trial was not just a religious inquisition — it was a **suppression of evolved consciousness by political-theological power**.

From a neuroscientific lens, this was the destruction of a mind operating at an advanced state of coherence. From a Qur'anic lens, it was the silencing of one who had witnessed truth within, and dared to speak it.

Legacy and Misuse

Ironically, many who claim to follow Hallaj today have turned his life into mysticism, miracle stories, and esoteric rituals — the very things he stood against. His *Ana al-Haqq* is quoted in poetry, sung in Sufi gatherings, but rarely understood in its original **neuro-cognitive and Qur'anic context.**

The real danger lies not in Hallaj's words, but in their **misuse by lower-consciousness minds** seeking popularity, not truth — a subject we will explore in later chapters.

Conclusion: Reclaiming Hallaj Through Science and Revelation

Mansoor Al-Hallaj was not a magician, mystic, or madman. He was a human being whose consciousness evolved to perceive unity, truth, and self-transcendence. His declaration *Ana al-Haqq* was not theological arrogance — it was the ultimate cognitive humility: the realization that the self, when stripped of ego, is not separate from truth.

By understanding Hallaj through the lenses of **neuroscience, psychology, and Qur'anic revelation**, we do not demystify him — we **restore him to**

reality. And reality, as both science and the Qur'an confirm, is far more profound than superstition could ever describe.

Chapter 2: What Did 'Ana al-Haqq' Mean?

"Say: The truth has come, and falsehood has vanished. Indeed, falsehood is bound to vanish." (Qur'an 17:81)

Introduction: Unpacking the Statement of a Conscious Mind

Among the most provocative statements ever uttered in Islamic intellectual history is the phrase "Ana al-Haqq" (أنا الحق), attributed to Mansoor Al-Hallaj. This statement has echoed for centuries through academic debates, religious polemics, poetic expressions, and political confrontations. It is often either idolized or demonized. However, the real depth and cognitive complexity behind this declaration are rarely examined from a rational, scientific, and Quranically grounded perspective. This chapter aims to unpack the literal, historical, psychological, and neuroscientific dimensions of the phrase "Ana al-Haqq," devoid of mystical jargon or esoteric assumptions.

Literal Translation and Semantic Analysis

The phrase "Ana al-Haqq" is composed of two Arabic words:

- **Ana** (أنا): This is the first-person singular pronoun, meaning "I am."
- **Al-Haqq** (الحق): This term is commonly translated as "The Truth," but its semantic range includes "reality," "justice," "right," and "ultimate fact."

In theological discourse, **Al-Haqq** is one of the 99 names of Allah, signifying the Absolute Reality. In secular Arabic usage, however, "al-Haqq" refers to that which is objectively true and just. When Mansoor Al-Hallaj said, "Ana al-Haqq," he was not saying "I am Allah" in a literal sense. Rather, he was asserting, in the language of advanced consciousness, that his personal identity had aligned with the universal truth that permeates existence.

From a modern cognitive standpoint, such alignment can be described as **non-dual awareness** — a state of consciousness in which the distinction between the observer and the observed collapses. The "I" (ego-self) dissolves, and what remains is a direct experience of truth or reality, not mediated by cultural, religious, or linguistic constructs.

Historical Reaction: Orthodoxy, Power, and Fear

To appreciate the gravity of Hallaj's statement, one must situate it within its historical context. Hallaj lived in the 9th and early 10th centuries during the Abbasid Caliphate, a time when Islamic jurisprudence and theology were heavily institutionalized. Religious scholars, particularly those aligned with political authority, acted as gatekeepers of orthodoxy.

The declaration "Ana al-Haqq" was heard by such scholars not through the lens of metaphysical depth or spiritual realization but as a political and theological rebellion. Claiming an attribute of Allah was interpreted as **shirk** (associating partners with God) or **hulul** (incarnationism), both capital offenses in Islamic law at the time.

The judiciary and clergy failed to discern the cognitive nuance of Hallaj's state. They saw a man stepping beyond the boundaries of allowable language. Rather than attempt to understand his mind, they framed his words as heresy and demanded his death.

The Neuroscientific Interpretation

In modern neuroscience, Hallaj's state of consciousness can be mapped onto what researchers call **self-transcendent experiences (STEs)**. These experiences, often reported by advanced meditators or individuals in intense states of reflection, involve a temporary suspension of the default mode network (DMN) in the brain, the area responsible for egoic self-reference.

When the DMN quiets, the individual often experiences a sense of unity with all that exists. There is no longer a distinction between "me" and "not me." In such states, people often describe themselves using universal terms: light, truth, being, or love. Hallaj's declaration, "I am the Truth," can be viewed in this light — as a direct cognitive realization of the interconnectedness of all things.

Importantly, this is not delusion or hallucination. On the contrary, studies using fMRI and EEG have confirmed that such states are often marked by increased gamma wave synchrony, suggesting heightened integration of neural activity across different brain regions. These are not signs of madness but of an advanced, coherent consciousness.

Qur'anic Validation of Cognitive Awakening

Contrary to the orthodox narrative, the Qur'an does not forbid self-realization or higher states of consciousness. In fact, it encourages introspection and awareness:

> *"We will show them Our signs in the horizons and within themselves until it becomes clear to them that it is the Truth."* (Qur'an 41:53)

This verse suggests that the realization of Truth (al-Haqq) is not confined to scripture or institutions but can occur "within themselves" — that is, within human consciousness. When Hallaj said "Ana al-Haqq," he may well have been one of those who reached this state through inner purification, reflection, and the dismantling of the ego.

The Qur'an also states:

> *"Indeed, We created man and We know what his soul whispers to him, and We are closer to him than [his] jugular vein."* (Qur'an 50:16)

This closeness suggests that divine truth is not distant but intimately embedded within human cognition. Realizing it, therefore, is not blasphemy — it is an advanced cognitive function.

The Misinterpretation by Religious Institutions

One of the tragic aspects of Hallaj's life is how his realization was distorted by those in power. Religious elites, threatened by any narrative outside their jurisdiction, weaponized theology to protect their authority. The same Qur'an that validated deep introspection and consciousness was used to silence someone who embodied its message.

The tendency to interpret high-conscious statements through low-conscious filters is a recurring theme in human history. When an evolved mind speaks from unity, ego-based minds perceive it as arrogance. When a person says "I am the Truth," they are not making a claim to power, but a surrender of the ego. But those who interpret this through the lens of control see it as competition or heresy.

The Role of Language: Expression Beyond Words

Human language is limited. It evolved primarily for survival and social organization, not for articulating transcendental states. When individuals like Hallaj experience unity with reality, they are often forced to use inadequate linguistic tools to convey the inexpressible.

Thus, statements like "Ana al-Haqq" should not be interpreted literally. They must be understood as linguistic attempts to express profound realizations. In neuroscience, this is called **semantic compression** — the collapsing of complex mental states into simplified expressions.

Religious orthodoxy, however, tends to interpret such statements through rigid, legalistic paradigms. The nuance is lost, and what was meant to describe a mental state becomes a theological scandal.

Ana al-Haqq as Cognitive Integration

From a psychological and neuroscientific viewpoint, we can reinterpret "Ana al-Haqq" as a state of **cognitive integration**. This term refers to the harmonization of different aspects of the self — emotional, intellectual, sensory — into a unified field of awareness. Such states are rare and usually result from years of inner discipline, self-inquiry, and reflection.

In integrated consciousness:

- The distinction between subject and object fades.
- The inner dialogue of the ego is silenced.
- Perception becomes direct and non-dualistic.

In this state, the self no longer says, "I observe the truth" but rather, "I am the truth," because the observer and the observed have merged.

Modern Implications: Why It Still Matters

In today's world, where science and religion often stand at odds, Hallaj's case offers a unique opportunity. His experience bridges the language of revelation with the findings of neuroscience. It provides a model for how human consciousness, when properly understood, can align with universal truths without resorting to mysticism or dogma.

Furthermore, reclaiming Hallaj through logic and evidence can serve as a counter-narrative to religious extremism and anti-scientific attitudes. It demonstrates that spirituality need not contradict science, and that the Qur'an, when interpreted through reason and evidence, aligns with the deepest structures of the human mind.

Conclusion: The Truth Within

"Ana al-Haqq" is not a claim of divine status but a cognitive milestone. It represents the point at which the personal self merges with objective reality — a state validated by both the Qur'an and modern neuroscience. Hallaj's declaration should not be dismissed as blasphemy or mysticism. It is a call to awaken, to integrate, and to realize that truth is not outside us, but within.

The tragedy of Mansoor Al-Hallaj is not just that he was executed. It is that his words have been buried under centuries of misinterpretation. As we move forward in this book, we will continue to explore how science and scripture together can help us reclaim not only Hallaj's legacy but also our own potential for consciousness and truth.

Chapter 3: Misinterpretations of Ana al-Haqq

Qur'anic Foundation vs. Cultural Mythology

The statement "Ana al-Haqq" (I am the Truth), attributed to Mansoor al-Hallaj, has sparked centuries of mystical reverence, accusations of blasphemy, and philosophical speculation. While many accept it as a Sufi proclamation of divine unity or spiritual intoxication, a closer analysis through the lenses of neuroscience and the Quran reveals that such interpretations have often diverged from rational understanding. This chapter attempts to dismantle the mythical constructs and miracle-laden accounts that have obfuscated the psychological and spiritual reality behind Hallaj's expression. It clarifies philosophical confusions that have led to cultism, blind devotion, and manipulation of religious consciousness.

The Rise of Mythical Sufism

The development of Sufi traditions in the medieval Islamic world provided fertile ground for mysticism. While early ascetics emphasized self-discipline and inner purification, later generations romanticized mystical states as divine miracles. Hallaj's cry "Ana al-Haqq" was thus gradually absorbed into a corpus of mythological storytelling. Instead of interpreting this statement as the result of deep introspective awareness, later Sufi circles began to treat it as an utterance of divinity itself. Some went so far as to consider Hallaj a martyr-saint who achieved literal union with God. Others surrounded his life with miracle stories—taming wild beasts, walking on water, speaking languages he had never learned—thus severing his thought from the logical realm and pushing it into hagiographical absurdity.

This mythologizing process served multiple psychological and political functions. It elevated charismatic leaders to near-divine status, gave rise to spiritual sectarianism, and created emotional rather than intellectual attachments. Such mythmaking distracted followers from the rational and ethical teachings at the heart of the Quran and Islam. In truth, the Quran never promotes supernatural mysticism; rather, it emphasizes reasoning (`aql), reflection (tafakkur), and insight (basirah).

Qur'an's Rejection of Human Deification

The Quran categorically denies any human claim to divinity. In Surah Al-Ma'idah (5:116), Allah addresses Jesus:

> "Did you say to the people, 'Take me and my mother as deities besides Allah'?" He will say, 'Exalted are You! It was not for me to say that to which I have no right.'"

If even Jesus, who was widely misunderstood as divine, is exonerated in the Quran from any claim to divinity, then the idea that Hallaj, a fallible human being, declared himself God must be critically reconsidered. Rather, "Ana al-Haqq" must be read within the psychological framework of heightened awareness—not divine identification.

The Neuroscience of Transcendent States

Modern neuroscience has made significant strides in mapping states of consciousness associated with transcendence, ego-dissolution, and self-realization. These states, often reached through meditation, intense focus, or even trauma, activate specific regions in the brain such as the prefrontal cortex and default mode network (DMN). During deep contemplative states, the DMN quiets down, allowing for a dissolution of the ego-bound self and a greater sense of connection with the universe.

Dr. Andrew Newberg, in his studies on mystical experience, noted that advanced meditators often describe a profound sense of unity with existence. Neuroscientifically, this is not a miracle but a state of the brain's capacity to move beyond ordinary thought patterns. What Hallaj likely experienced was an advanced state of consciousness in which the boundaries between self and existence blurred—leading to the declaration, not that he was God, but that his self (Ana) was inseparable from Truth (Al-Haqq). This interpretation aligns both with logic and Quranic monotheism.

Sufi Misinterpretations: Emotionalism Over Reason

Many later Sufis, especially post-Hallaj, began to treat the statement "Ana al-Haqq" not as a cognitive insight but as a sign of divine incarnation or fana (annihilation into God). While fana is often discussed metaphorically in early Sufism, it was increasingly taken literally, leading to dangerous theological confusion. The notion that a person can be "absorbed" into God is directly at odds with Quranic tawheed (unity of God), which affirms that God is wholly distinct from creation (Surah Ash-Shura 42:11: "There is nothing like unto Him.").

Emotionalism in spirituality, while potentially useful for inspiration, becomes harmful when it overrides logic and leads to superstition. The mystical elevation of saints and Sufi leaders has often resulted in shrine worship, saint veneration, and the formation of spiritual cults that manipulate the masses under the guise of secret knowledge. Hallaj's insight into consciousness has thus been distorted into a doctrine of divine possession, stripping it of its intellectual value.

Miracle-Based Narratives: A Tool for Power

The portrayal of Hallaj's life is filled with unsubstantiated miracle stories that cannot be verified and often contradict Quranic principles. These stories include claims that he resurrected birds, spoke with the dead, or transformed his body at will. Such narratives mirror the miracle tales often talked about saints in Christianity, Hinduism, and other traditions—tales that foster emotional loyalty rather than critical thought.

From a sociopolitical perspective, miracle-stories serve to legitimize spiritual authority. A person declared capable of miracles is presumed to have a divine endorsement, making followers less likely to question their teachings. This can and has been abused by charismatic leaders to amass wealth, power, and control. The real revolution in Hallaj's thought was not supernatural—it was rational and psychological. By interpreting "Ana al-Haqq" as the utterance of a mind fully attuned to existential truth, we return the phrase to its rightful domain: a scientific understanding of consciousness and cognition.

Philosophical Confusion: Identity vs. Ontology

A major source of confusion in interpreting Hallaj's statement lies in the misunderstanding of identity. When Hallaj said, "I am the Truth," he was not making an ontological claim that he *is* God. Rather, he was expressing a psychological state in which his self was aligned with truth, reality, and essence.

Consider a scientist who, after decades of research, exclaims, "I have become knowledge." Clearly, this is metaphorical. It reflects identity *with* a field, not identity *as* an essence. Likewise, "Ana al-Haqq" is best read as "My consciousness has dissolved into the reality of existence" or "I perceive only Truth within and without." This interpretation avoids both theological error and philosophical nonsense.

In Quranic language, this state is one of *tazkiyah* (purification) and *yaqeen* (certainty), not divinity. Surah Al-Hujurat (49:13) says, "Indeed, the most noble of you in the sight of Allah is the most righteous." Righteousness, not mystical union, is the measure of spiritual success. Hallaj's righteousness lay in his pursuit of truth, not in the mythical powers attributed to him.

Modern Applications and Ethical Clarity

In a world overwhelmed with spiritual exploitation, the misinterpretation of mystical language continues to enable fraud, sectarianism, and social division. Self-proclaimed messiahs and gurus continue to cite misunderstood mystics like Hallaj to justify their superiority. By clarifying "Ana al-Haqq" through neuroscience and Quranic rationality, we inoculate society against the misuse of spiritual language.

Hallaj did not demand worship. He did not declare a new religion. He was a man of profound introspection who reached a state of alignment with truth. He expressed it with poetic brevity, which became a victim of cultural and religious distortion.

Conclusion: Returning to Truth

To free Hallaj from myth and return him to meaning, we must strip away the legends and look closely at the human brain, the Quranic framework, and the psychological essence of his statement. "Ana al-Haqq" is not a divine claim; it is a human awakening—a glimpse into the highest capacity of the human mind to perceive universal truth. When understood correctly, it leads not to deification but to humility, not to cultism but to clarity.

The next chapter will explore the neuroscience of self-transcendence and how this psychological transformation may have shaped Hallaj's consciousness.

Chapter 4: Haqq in the Quran: Meaning and Attributes

"And say: The truth has come, and falsehood has vanished. Surely, falsehood is ever bound to vanish." — Qur'an 17:81

The phrase "Ana al-Haqq" uttered by Mansoor Al-Hallaj has perplexed scholars for centuries. To understand its intended meaning through a purely scientific and Quranic lens, one must dissect the meaning of *Haqq* itself. This chapter delves into the concept of *Al-Haqq* as defined in the Qur'an, clarifying that it is not associated with any individual but represents the ultimate truth — the reality that governs existence. Furthermore, we will critically assess the attribution of the so-called "99 names of Allah," a concept often assumed to be Quranic but actually rooted in Hadith traditions and theological elaborations post-Qur'an.

1. Haqq in the Quran: The Foundation of Truth

The word *Haqq* in Arabic stems from the root "ḥa-qa-qa" ح ق ق), meaning to be real, to be true, or to exist in actual reality. In the Qur'an, *Al-Haqq* is used frequently as a descriptor for divine truth, cosmic order, and the unwavering principles that govern life and existence.

Examples of Quranic usage:

- *"That is because Allah is the Truth (Al-Haqq), and what they call upon besides Him is falsehood."* (Qur'an 22:62)
- *"Allah is the Creator of everything, and He is, over all things, Disposer of affairs. To Him belong the keys of the heavens and the earth. And those who disbelieve in the verses of Allah — it is they who are the losers."* (Qur'an 39:62-63)

In these verses, *Haqq* is not anthropomorphized but presented as the immutable, observable reality. It refers to the consistent, measurable laws of nature, morality, and existence that are self-evident and indestructible.

2. Haqq is Not a Person: Debunking Theological

Misappropriation

The confusion arose when mystics or followers of later Sufi sects began interpreting "Ana al-Haqq" as a claim to divinity. This idea directly conflicts with the Qur'anic assertion that Allah is incomparable and beyond anthropomorphic association:

- *"There is nothing like unto Him, and He is the Hearing, the Seeing."* (Qur'an 42:11)

If Haqq were to be attributed to a person, it would mean that the totality of ultimate truth, justice, and universal order could be contained in a single human — a concept fundamentally incompatible with Quranic monotheism and the natural limits of human consciousness.

Hallaj's utterance, as this book aims to establish, was a philosophical metaphor rooted in his personal conscious state and not a divine claim. The later mythologizing of his words distanced them from their likely intention — that the self is a mirror to truth, not a vessel of it.

3. Haqq as a Cosmic Principle in Physics and Consciousness

In the modern scientific worldview, *Haqq* could be equated to fundamental constants, physical laws, and universal principles that uphold the integrity of reality. Just as gravity or the speed of light are unchanging truths in physics, the Qur'an's references to *Haqq* indicate foundational realities that do not depend on human recognition or interpretation.

- *"We did not create the heavens and the earth and what is between them except in truth and for an appointed term."* (Qur'an 46:3)

The term *bil-Haqq* (with the truth) is used here to signify that creation itself was not arbitrary but structured, lawful, and meaningful. This aligns with our contemporary understanding of the universe as an ordered system governed by consistent patterns and feedback mechanisms.

4. The Myth of the "99 Names of Allah"

One of the most popular theological expansions upon the identity of Allah is the so-called *Asma'ul Husna* or the 99 beautiful names of Allah. These names, such as *Ar-Rahman* (The Most Merciful), *Al-Malik* (The King), and *Al-Haqq* (The Truth), are often presented as if they are a Quranic framework. However, this is a misconception.

The Qur'an does mention attributes of Allah, but it never specifies that there are exactly 99 names, nor does it enumerate them in a list. The idea of the 99 names comes primarily from Hadith literature, such as the famous narration in Sahih Muslim:

- *"Allah has 99 names, one hundred less one; whoever memorizes them will enter Paradise."* (Sahih Muslim, Book 35, Hadith 6475)

It is essential to note that this Hadith has multiple versions and inconsistent listings of these names. The Quran does refer to several attributes (e.g., *Ar-Rahman*, *Ar-Raheem*, *Al-Khaliq*), but these appear contextually and not as part of a systematized list.

The institutionalization of the 99 names occurred much later, influenced by schools of theology, jurisprudence, and Sufism. It became a part of liturgical and devotional practices, not Quranic instruction.

5. Why This Matters

The insertion of non-Quranic concepts into public belief systems has led to widespread confusion about the nature of Allah, and consequently, the nature of truth itself. If *Haqq* is misunderstood as a personal attribute that can be owned or claimed, it opens the door to blasphemy, mysticism, or personality cults.

More dangerously, this misinterpretation creates hierarchical models in religion, where certain individuals are treated as semi-divine or infallible — a practice that has led to sectarianism, spiritual exploitation, and political manipulation in the name of religion.

The Quran consistently fights against such distortions:

- *"Say: I am only a man like you, to whom has been revealed that your god is One God. So whoever would hope for the meeting with his Lord — let him do righteous work and not associate in the worship of his Lord anyone."* (Qur'an 18:110)

This verse affirms the human status of prophets and thinkers, asserting that the only thing that elevates a person is revelation (truth) — not any inherent divinity or proximity to *Haqq*.

6. Reconciling Consciousness and Haqq

From a neuroscience perspective, the perception of truth is a complex cognitive function. It involves higher-order brain functions including reasoning, pattern recognition, emotional integration, and ethical judgment. When a person, such as Hallaj, attains a state of heightened consciousness or cognitive integration, they may *perceive* themselves as aligning with fundamental truths. This can give rise to the powerful subjective experience that "I am truth."

However, subjective perception is not ontological reality. Just because a person feels united with cosmic truth doesn't mean they *are* the cosmic truth. Hallaj's statement is best understood as a poetic description of an altered mental state rather than a metaphysical claim.

The Qur'an, while acknowledging elevated mental states (e.g., *qalbun salim* — a sound mind), never equates this with godhood. It maintains a strict boundary between the Creator and the created:

- *"They have not appraised Allah with true appraisal."* (Qur'an 39:67)

The act of misattributing divinity to humans, even if unintentionally, leads to conceptual idolatry (*shirk*), which is condemned repeatedly in the Qur'an.

Conclusion

To truly understand *Ana al-Haqq*, one must first understand what *Haqq* is — not from mystical tales, not from Hadith narratives about 99 names, but from the source that claims to be *al-Furqan* (The Criterion): the Qur'an.

Haqq is not a person, not a feeling, and not an experience. It is the eternal, unchanging, empirical truth embedded in the structure of the universe and morality — a truth described, not personified, by the Qur'an. The misinterpretation of *Haqq* and the false elevation of Hadith-based concepts like the 99 names have only served to cloud the clarity of divine truth.

Returning to the Qur'an is not just a religious act; it is an intellectual necessity for any sincere seeker of truth. As this chapter has demonstrated, *Al-Haqq* is an anchor of rational monotheism — untethered from mysticism, sustained by revelation, and affirmed by reason.

Chapter 5: The Human Self (Nafs) in the Quran

"And I do not acquit myself. Indeed, the self (nafs) is inclined to evil, except the one on whom my Lord has mercy. Indeed, my Lord is Forgiving and Merciful."
— Surah Yusuf (12:53)

Introduction: Revisiting the Concept of the Self

In the field of psychology and neuroscience, the concept of the self has been widely debated. Modern science attempts to locate the self in the cognitive patterns of the brain, particularly the prefrontal cortex, responsible for self-awareness, moral reasoning, and decision-making. However, the Quran predates modern psychological models with a sophisticated and layered understanding of the self, known in Arabic as *Nafs*. In this chapter, we explore the Quranic model of *Nafs* and how it aligns with, and sometimes surpasses, modern scientific thought about the human ego, self-regulation, and consciousness.

The Three Stages of Nafs in the Quran

The Quran introduces three distinct stages or conditions of the human self:

1. **Nafs al-Ammarah (The Commanding Self)**
2. **Nafs al-Lawwama (The Self-Reproaching Self)**
3. **Nafs al-Mutma'innah (The Tranquil Self)**

Each of these stages corresponds not only to a level of moral and spiritual maturity but also reflects a neurological and psychological transformation in the human brain.

Nafs al-Ammarah: The Commanding Self

The term *Nafs al-Ammarah* comes from Surah Yusuf (12:53), where Prophet Yusuf acknowledges the innate tendency of the human self to command towards evil unless tempered by divine consciousness.

"Indeed, the self (nafs) commands to evil (ammaratun bis-su') ..."

This stage of the self is characterized by primal instincts, immediate gratification, selfish desires, and a lack of restraint. In neuroscience, this correlates with impulsive behavior linked to the amygdala and limbic system, areas of the brain responsible for emotional response and basic drives. When the prefrontal cortex (which governs reasoning and control) is underdeveloped or inactive, the limbic system dominates, leading to irrational and self-destructive choices.

Scientific Parallel: The Nafs al-Ammarah corresponds to what neuroscientists describe as the dominance of the "reptilian brain" and the limbic circuitry, where immediate survival instincts override long-term planning or ethical reflection. Such individuals may lack empathy, show high reactivity to stimuli, and struggle with delayed gratification.

Quranic Insight: The Quran does not condemn this stage as inherently evil but identifies it as the base nature that every human must transcend. It is the raw material of the soul that can either remain in darkness or be refined through awareness, discipline, and connection with *Haqq*—the absolute truth.

Nafs al-Lawwama: The Self-Reproaching Self

Mentioned in Surah Al-Qiyamah (75:2), *Nafs al-Lawwama* represents a higher level of self-awareness.

"And I swear by the self-reproaching soul (Nafs al-Lawwama)."

This stage marks the awakening of conscience. The individual begins to recognize moral failures, feels remorse, and experiences internal conflict. It is a transitional stage between impulsive living and conscious self-regulation. From a neuroscientific perspective, this reflects the growing activity in the prefrontal cortex, especially in regions involved in moral judgment and self-evaluation.

Scientific Parallel: At this stage, the individual demonstrates metacognition—the ability to think about one's own thinking. The anterior cingulate cortex plays a role in error detection and conflict monitoring, and is activated when a person reflects on mistakes. This aligns with the *Lawwama* stage, where one criticizes oneself internally for failing to act according to higher ideals.

Quranic Insight: This phase is seen as a sign of moral and psychological growth. The Quran values this stage by swearing an oath by it—a method used in the Quran to emphasize importance. The presence of guilt and self-reproach is not viewed negatively but as a doorway to refinement.

Nafs al-Mutma'innah: The Tranquil Self

Finally, the most refined and spiritually evolved state of the human self is described in Surah Al-Fajr (89:27-30):

"O tranquil soul (Nafs al-Mutma'innah), return to your Lord well-pleased and pleasing [to Him]."

This is the state of inner peace, moral certainty, and alignment with truth (*Haqq*). The individual no longer experiences cognitive dissonance between desire and duty. In neuroscience, this correlates with states of neurochemical balance and sustained mindfulness. Long-term meditators and those with high emotional intelligence often show stable brain patterns in the prefrontal cortex and reduced reactivity in the amygdala.

Scientific Parallel: This stage mirrors the concept of emotional regulation, neuroplasticity, and self-mastery. Studies in neuroscience show that people with high emotional intelligence and self-control exhibit stronger connectivity between the prefrontal cortex and limbic areas. They are less likely to be overwhelmed by stress or fear and are able to sustain focus and compassion.

Quranic Insight: The tranquility of this soul is not a product of ignorance or illusion but of deep alignment with reality, logic, and ethical behavior. It is a mind in harmony with the universe and with itself. It has transcended egoic desires and emotional volatility.

A Model of Self-Control and Ethical Maturity

What emerges from the Quranic framework is a powerful model of the human psyche. Rather than placing humans in a binary of good vs. evil, the Quran presents a developmental model. Each level of *nafs* is a psychological milestone that can be cultivated through discipline, awareness, and truth-based living.

This model rejects fatalism and instead promotes personal responsibility. It aligns closely with the cognitive-behavioral model of modern psychology where thoughts shape behaviors and conscious restructuring of belief systems leads to moral transformation.

Beyond Sufism: Rational Clarity on Nafs

In later Islamic traditions, particularly within Sufism, the concept of *nafs* was expanded into seven or more stages, many of which were filled with mystical and speculative elements. However, these elaborations, while influential in the history of Islamic thought, often departed from the core logic and simplicity of the Quran.

Our purpose is not to invalidate these traditions but to refocus on the Quran itself, which presents *nafs* in a manner consistent with both logic and science. The Quranic understanding does not require allegorical interpretations or supernatural concepts. It treats the human being as a conscious, evolving entity capable of reaching states of clarity and peace through rational alignment with the truth (*Haqq*).

Final Reflection: The Self as a Site of Evolution

The human *nafs* is not static. It is a dynamic, evolving structure deeply tied to consciousness, morality, and cognitive function. By analyzing the Quranic descriptions of the *nafs* through the lens of neuroscience, we discover a compelling harmony between revelation and reason.

The Quranic model offers a road map of ethical and psychological evolution, grounded in natural human experience rather than dogma. It demands that individuals work through their inner conflicts—not through superstition or mystical escape, but through conscious effort, reflection, and alignment with *Haqq*, the ultimate truth.

In the context of Mansoor Al-Hallaj's "Ana al-Haqq," understanding *nafs* is crucial. The self that can truly utter such a claim, free from ego and illusion, must have passed through all stages—tamed the commanding self, struggled with the reproaching self, and finally arrived at the tranquil self that mirrors truth itself.

The journey of *nafs* is the journey of consciousness unfolding from darkness to light, from chaos to coherence, from desire to divine alignment.

Chapter 6: The 'Self' and its Annihilation (Fanā) in Quranic Language

"Every soul shall taste death. Then to Us you will be returned." — (Quran 29:57)

"Whoever purifies it (the self) has succeeded, and whoever corrupts it has failed." — (Quran 91:9-10)

Introduction: The Concept of 'Fana'

In classical Sufi literature, the term *Fanā* (فناء) has often been interpreted as "the annihilation of the self"—a spiritual phase in which the ego (Nafs) dissolves into the Divine Reality (Haqq). However, this idea has been largely wrapped in metaphor, mysticism, and poetic abstraction. In this chapter, we aim to reclaim and redefine the concept of *Fanā* using purely Quranic language and scientific reasoning—stripping away esoteric mysticism and approaching it through the lens of consciousness studies and self-awareness.

The Quran, while never using the specific term *Fanā*, repeatedly encourages the transcendence of ego and the alignment of the self with truth (Haqq). In doing so, it describes a psychological transformation that mirrors what neuroscientists today refer to as "ego dissolution" or "ego death," a process through which the illusion of a fixed, isolated self is replaced by a broader, interconnected awareness.

Understanding the Self: Neuroscience Meets Quran

To comprehend what the Quran implies by self-annihilation, we must first revisit what the modern sciences say about the concept of the 'self.'

Neuroscience has demonstrated that the brain constructs the "self" as an adaptive narrative—a functional fiction maintained by the default mode network (DMN), a group of interconnected regions of the brain that becomes active during introspective thought. This self-narrative is tied closely to memories, desires, cultural conditioning, and internal dialogue.

From the Quranic perspective, this constructed self is the *Nafs*—an entity that fluctuates between base instincts (*Nafs-e-Ammarah*), self-reproach and ethical struggle (*Nafs-e-Lawwama*), and inner peace or surrender

(*Nafs-e-Mutmainnah*). The journey of human development in the Quran is to move from the first stage toward the third. This trajectory is not a mystical merging with God but rather a conscious evolution toward alignment with Haqq—the truth, the reality, the universal order.

The Illusion of the Ego and the Reality of Haqq

In both neuroscience and the Quran, the self is not a fixed identity. Rather, it is dynamic, shaped by internal and external experiences. The Quran recognizes this malleability:

"By the soul and the One who proportioned it, then inspired it with its wickedness and its righteousness. Indeed, he succeeds who purifies it, and he fails who corrupts it." — (Quran 91:7–10)

This purification is not about mystical experiences; it is about consciously shedding illusions—attachments to pride, desires, false beliefs, and the illusion of separateness. In this light, *Fanā* is not metaphysical disappearance but a psychological reorientation—a collapse of the illusion of the ego and a reestablishment of self on the basis of universal truth.

Neuroscientifically, experiences of ego dissolution often occur during intense meditative states, near-death experiences, or the use of psychedelics (though the Quran does not endorse or refer to any drug use). These moments reveal the fragility of the ego's narrative and open the individual to an experience of self not bounded by personal history or identity. Such insights mirror the Quranic call to transcend the Nafs and awaken to Haqq.

Fanā as Cognitive Surrender to Truth

When the Quran calls for *Islam*—submission—it is not asking for blind obedience to rituals, but a surrender of the ego's delusions to the reality of universal truth. In other words, *Fanā* is the death of self-delusion.

"And do not follow [your own] desire, as it will lead you away from the path of Allah. Indeed, those who wander astray from the path of Allah will have a severe punishment for having forgotten the Day of Account." — (Quran 38:26)

This verse highlights that the ego's desires are misleading. The path to truth lies in disidentifying with selfish impulses and aligning with the reality of interconnected existence. Here, *Fanā* emerges not as annihilation in a mystical sense, but as a rational process of letting go of personal falsehoods.

This surrender is supported by neuroscience. Studies on mindfulness and meditation show that when individuals quiet their inner monologue and reduce ego-related activity in the brain's DMN, they report heightened states of clarity, empathy, and unity—experiences that can be likened to the Quranic *Nafs-e-Mutmainnah*, the tranquil self.

From Self-Assertion to Self-Realization

Hallaj's statement *Ana al-Haqq* (I am the Truth) can now be understood not as a claim to divinity, but as a profound realization: when the ego is dissolved, what remains is awareness aligned with truth. The individual no longer sees themselves as separate, superior, or in control, but as part of an unfolding reality governed by truth.

"Indeed, those who say, 'Our Lord is Allah,' and then remain steadfast—no fear will be upon them, nor will they grieve." — (Quran 46:13)

This verse implies a psychological state of stability that arises when the self recognizes its grounding in truth. It is not the loss of identity but the purification of identity—a cognitive and moral shift from self-centeredness to truth-centeredness.

The Fanā Process in Three Stages (Scientific and Quranic Integration)

1. Recognition of Illusion (Cognitive Awakening): This corresponds to *Nafs-e-Lawwama*. The individual begins to observe the ego's patterns, questioning motives, reactions, and beliefs. Scientifically, this stage is marked by increased activity in the anterior cingulate cortex, which governs introspection and error detection.

2. Deconstruction of the Ego (Neural Rewiring): The individual, through continuous self-observation and surrender to ethical truth, reduces ego dominance. Meditation studies show that the DMN becomes less dominant in long-term practitioners. Quranic verses that stress *Tazkiyah* (purification) encourage this rewiring.

3. Merging with Truth (Cognitive Alignment): This is not loss of self but redefinition. The self becomes a mirror of Haqq—not claiming divinity but living in alignment with divine attributes like justice, mercy, and wisdom. This is *Nafs-e-Mutmainnah*.

"O tranquil soul, return to your Lord—well-pleased and pleasing [to Him]. So enter among My servants and enter My Paradise." — (Quran 89:27–30)

This "Paradise" is not necessarily post-death. It is also the state of the mind that has found peace through alignment with truth.

Conclusion: Ego Death is Self-Realization, Not Erasure

In conclusion, the concept of *Fanā* in the Quran is neither a mystical union with God nor a metaphysical extinction. It is the logical consequence of deep psychological introspection and spiritual awakening. It is the movement from selfishness to truthfulness, from ego to awareness, from illusion to reality.

The Quran is not a book of esotericism. It is a rational, psychological, and ethical guide to human transformation. Through its clear references to *Nafs*, *Haqq*, and *Tazkiyah*, it outlines a process by which the false self is transcended—not to become God, but to become truly human. This is the real meaning of *Fanā*: the ego dissolves, and the truth remains.

Chapter 7: What is Consciousness? A Scientific Overview

"And He gave you hearing, sight, and hearts (consciousness); little thanks do you give." — Qur'an 32:9

Consciousness is one of the most profound and elusive phenomena studied in science and philosophy. It is at once the most familiar and the most mysterious feature of human existence. From the whisper of self-awareness to the complex interplay of thoughts, emotions, memories, and intentions, consciousness defines the human experience. Yet despite centuries of inquiry, the scientific community still grapples with fundamental questions: What is consciousness? How does it arise? Can it be quantified or explained through physical processes alone?

This chapter explores the evolving scientific understanding of consciousness. It examines the "hard problem" of consciousness as posed by philosophers, reviews contemporary scientific models—including the works of Roger Penrose, Giulio Tononi, and Christof Koch—and links these to broader discussions relevant to the Qur'anic conception of the human self.

The Hard Problem of Consciousness

The term "hard problem of consciousness" was coined by philosopher David Chalmers in the 1990s. It distinguishes between the "easy problems" of consciousness—such as understanding how the brain processes information or controls behavior—and the hard problem: explaining subjective experience.

Why does information processing in the brain feel like anything from the inside? How do physical processes give rise to qualia—the internal, subjective component of perception? For instance, why does the experience of seeing the color red feel as it does? Why is pain painful? These questions elude purely mechanistic explanations.

While many scientists have proposed that consciousness is an emergent property of brain complexity, this view fails to resolve how physical systems acquire subjectivity. The hard problem exposes the limits of reductionist materialism and challenges the adequacy of classical physics in explaining the conscious mind.

Neural Correlates of Consciousness (NCC)

Scientific research has sought to identify the neural correlates of consciousness—the specific brain states or structures that correspond with conscious experience. Technologies such as EEG, fMRI, and PET scans have enabled researchers to observe the brain in various states: waking, dreaming, meditating, and under anesthesia.

Some consistent findings include:

- The prefrontal cortex plays a crucial role in higher-order thinking and self-awareness.
- The thalamus acts as a relay station, integrating sensory input with conscious attention.
- The default mode network (DMN) is active during introspection and autobiographical memory.

However, identifying correlations does not equal explanation. While we can track where and when consciousness-related activity occurs, we still do not know *why* it feels like something to be in that state. This unresolved gap remains central to consciousness research.

Roger Penrose: Quantum Consciousness

One of the boldest and most controversial theories of consciousness comes from Sir Roger Penrose, a mathematical physicist known for his work with Stephen Hawking on black holes. Penrose argues that consciousness cannot be explained by classical physics or algorithmic processes alone.

He posits that consciousness arises from quantum processes occurring in microtubules—tiny structures within neurons. Together with anesthesiologist Stuart Hameroff, Penrose developed the Orch-OR (Orchestrated Objective Reduction) theory. According to this model:

- Microtubules enable quantum coherence within the brain.

- These quantum states collapse into definite conscious experiences.
- Consciousness is thus linked to fundamental quantum laws, not just neural computation.

This theory, while speculative and contested, attempts to bridge the gap between physics and subjective awareness. It suggests that consciousness may be embedded in the fabric of the universe—a view that resonates with certain metaphysical interpretations of Qur'anic verses such as *"He is closer to you than your jugular vein"* (Qur'an 50:16).

Giulio Tononi: Integrated Information Theory (IIT)

Giulio Tononi's Integrated Information Theory (IIT) offers a mathematical and phenomenological framework for understanding consciousness. The central idea is that consciousness corresponds to the capacity of a system to integrate information in a unified way.

Key principles of IIT:

- **Information**: Consciousness requires differentiated states—different thoughts, sensations, or perceptions.
- **Integration**: Consciousness is not fragmented; it is unified. All parts of the experience are integrated into a whole.
- **Φ (Phi)**: A numerical measure of a system's consciousness. High Phi means high integration, and hence, higher consciousness.

IIT does not require a brain or even biology per se; theoretically, any system with sufficient information integration could be conscious. This opens philosophical questions about machine consciousness and panpsychism. IIT suggests that consciousness is not an all-or-nothing phenomenon but exists in degrees.

Christof Koch: Searching for the Neural Signature

Christof Koch, a former collaborator with Francis Crick, focuses on finding the minimal mechanisms that give rise to conscious experience. He advocates for a scientific approach that is empirically grounded yet open to philosophical complexity.

Koch agrees with Tononi's IIT but emphasizes the importance of distinguishing levels of consciousness:

- Wakeful, responsive consciousness (normal human state)
- Dreaming consciousness (active brain, altered sensory input)
- Minimal consciousness (coma, anesthesia)

Koch's research supports the idea that consciousness correlates with the level of brain integration and feedback loops. For example, recurrent activity between the thalamus and cortex seems crucial for maintaining conscious awareness.

Consciousness and the Brain: What We Know So Far

Despite the gaps, neuroscience has made progress in identifying some key characteristics of consciousness:

1. **Complexity**: Conscious experience emerges from a vast network of neurons operating in dynamic synchrony.
2. **Plasticity**: The brain can change its conscious states through meditation, trauma, drugs, or training.
3. **Continuity and Unity**: Consciousness has a flowing, unified quality even though it is built from multiple sub-processes.
4. **Subjectivity**: No external observer can fully access another's conscious experience; it remains first-person.

While neural correlates and quantum models provide pieces of the puzzle, none have fully solved the hard problem. This has led many scientists and thinkers to consider consciousness not as a by-product of brain activity, but as a fundamental aspect of reality.

The Qur'anic Perspective on Consciousness

The Qur'an does not use the modern term "consciousness," but it frequently refers to *qalb* (mind/heart), *sadr* (inner self), *nafs* (self), and *ruḥ* (spirit/breath of life)—all of which contribute to a model of layered human awareness.

Consider the verse:

> *"And We breathed into him of Our spirit (ruḥ)..."* — Qur'an 15:29

This implies a divine spark or dimension to human life beyond mere biology. The Qur'an presents humans as beings endowed with faculties of perception, reflection, and choice:

> *"Indeed, in that are signs for a people who reflect (yatafakkarūn)."* — Qur'an 30:21

In other verses, consciousness is tied to moral responsibility and self-awareness. The ability to distinguish right from wrong is seen not just as a cognitive function but as a spiritual and moral awareness rooted in the self (nafs).

> *"Indeed, the nafs is prone to command evil—except those upon whom my Lord has mercy."* — Qur'an 12:53

This aligns closely with psychological and neuroscientific understandings of the "conscious self" as a regulatory system balancing instinct, emotion, and reason.

Conclusion: Bridging the Scientific and Quranic View

The scientific exploration of consciousness reveals a deeply complex, multi-layered phenomenon that defies simple explanation. From the neural synchrony of brain regions to the quantum behavior of microtubules, the search for the seat of consciousness reflects the immense sophistication of the human mind.

Qur'anic descriptions, though using different language, also recognize the multi-dimensional nature of human awareness. The concepts of *nafs*, *ruḥ*, and *qalb* point toward a system of perception, self-reflection, and divine connection that science is only beginning to map.

Ultimately, consciousness may not be reducible to physical substrates alone. As science advances, it may increasingly validate what the Qur'an suggested centuries ago: that the essence of human awareness is tied to something deeper, something not limited to matter or machine. Whether through neural integration or quantum coherence, consciousness remains the doorway to understanding what it means to be truly human.

Chapter 8: The Illusion of the Self

"Have they not reflected within themselves? Allah created the heavens and the earth and whatever is between them for a purpose and an appointed term."
(Qur'an 30:8)

The Sense of Self – A Cognitive Construction

The question of what constitutes the "self" has long occupied scholars, philosophers, and scientists alike. In theology, it is often assumed that the self is a soul, a divine imprint residing within the human body. In neuroscience, however, the self is increasingly viewed as an emergent property—a construct of complex brain processes that gives rise to the subjective experience of "I" or ego. This chapter aims to explain how the brain constructs the illusion of a unified self and how this idea harmonizes with Qur'anic teachings that warn against egoic delusion. We will explore the neurological systems responsible for this phenomenon, particularly the Default Mode Network (DMN), and link these ideas to the Qur'anic understanding of self-awareness, accountability, and transcendence.

1. The Illusion of Unity: How the Brain Creates "I"

Contrary to common belief, there is no central command center in the brain where the self resides. Instead, the self is a narrative construct produced by various interconnected regions of the brain. When we say "I am," we are essentially narrating a story generated by brain functions that integrate memory, sensory information, social context, and personal goals.

Neuroscientific evidence supports this view through research on split-brain patients. When the corpus callosum (the connection between the two hemispheres of the brain) is severed, the two sides of the brain can function independently, often unaware of each other's intentions or perceptions. Despite this, patients still report a continuous sense of "self," though sometimes inconsistent between hemispheres. This suggests that the self is not a fixed entity but a continuous, adaptive narrative constructed by the brain.

2. Default Mode Network: The Home of the Ego

The Default Mode Network (DMN) has become a focal point in understanding the neurological basis of the self. The DMN consists of brain regions such as the medial prefrontal cortex, posterior cingulate cortex, and angular gyrus, which are active when the mind is at rest and not focused on the external environment.

DMN activity is associated with mind-wandering, daydreaming, and self-referential thought. It is the brain's mechanism for constructing a continuous sense of self across time. When people recall past experiences, imagine future events, or judge their own and others' behaviors, the DMN is highly active.

Interestingly, excessive DMN activity has been linked with depression, anxiety, and egocentric thought patterns. This has implications for spiritual practices as well; meditation and focused attention practices—whether religious or secular—have been shown to quiet the DMN, leading to what some describe as "ego dissolution." This supports the idea that ego is not essential, but a temporary mental state.

3. The Self as a Predictive Model

In cognitive neuroscience, the brain is increasingly seen as a prediction engine. According to predictive processing models, the brain constantly generates hypotheses about incoming sensory data and updates them based on error signals. The sense of self is similarly modeled: it is the brain's prediction of who "I" am in any given moment.

These predictions are informed by a lifetime of experiences and learning. The brain maintains a model of the body (proprioception), of social identity (cultural and relational roles), and of continuity across time (memory). This model is deeply ingrained but can be altered through trauma, psychological treatment, or spiritual experience.

From this perspective, the self is not a thing but a process—a dynamic simulation maintained by neural systems for the sake of biological survival and social integration.

4. Qur'anic Reflections on the Illusory Self

The Qur'an repeatedly emphasizes the dangers of nafs al-ammārah (the commanding ego) and the need for purification of the self:

> "Indeed, the self (nafs) is prone to evil except for those upon whom my Lord has mercy."
>
> (Qur'an 12:53)

This aligns with the scientific insight that the self is not a fixed divine core but a set of tendencies that can mislead, dominate, and corrupt unless trained or transformed. The Qur'an recognizes multiple levels of the self—commanding, reproaching, and peaceful—indicating that selfhood is a spectrum of consciousness, not a binary state.

> "By the soul and He who proportioned it, and inspired it with discernment between its right and wrong—he has succeeded who purifies it, and he has failed who corrupts it."
>
> (Qur'an 91:7-10)

This notion of purification (tazkiyah) resonates with the idea that ego (as generated by the DMN and self-referential systems) is not the ultimate self but a superficial layer that must be transcended.

5. Ego Dissolution and Mystical Experience: A Neuroscientific Link

When individuals undergo intense mystical or meditative experiences, they often report a loss of self—a sense of unity with all that exists, or merging with a universal consciousness. Neuroscience explains these experiences through temporary shutdowns or reorganizations of the DMN. Psychedelic substances like psilocybin and LSD, as well as deep meditation, have been shown to decrease DMN activity, often resulting in experiences of ego death or oneness.

While this has often been described in spiritual or mystical terms, the underlying mechanisms can be scientifically studied. Brain imaging studies show a reduction in neural connectivity between brain regions associated with self-reference. This creates a sense of boundary dissolution, where the individual no longer perceives themselves as separate from their environment.

Interestingly, these experiences are often interpreted as deeply meaningful, morally enlightening, and transformative. They result in greater feelings of compassion, humility, and connection—values echoed in the Qur'anic description of the purified soul (nafs al-mutma'innah).

> "O tranquil soul, return to your Lord, pleased and pleasing. Enter among My servants. Enter My Paradise."
>
> (Qur'an 89:27–30)

6. Implications: Humility, Morality, and Transcendence

Understanding that the self is a neurological construction rather than an absolute entity has profound moral and spiritual implications. It shifts our understanding of human flaws from being inherent sins to being cognitive distortions. Pride, greed, and hatred are not demonic forces but misaligned predictions and feedback loops in the brain.

Moreover, it reinforces the need for practices—spiritual, psychological, and social—that can help individuals realign their inner narrative with higher truths. The Qur'an repeatedly calls for *tadhakkur* (remembrance), *fikr* (reflection), and *tazkiyah* (purification), all of which serve to quiet the false self and reorient the individual toward reality (Haqq).

7. The Death of the False Self: A Qur'an-Neuroscience Convergence

In light of both Qur'anic language and neuroscience, ego death or the "illusion of the self" is not annihilation but liberation. It is the collapse of a false mental structure in favor of deeper, more authentic awareness. The Prophet Muhammad (peace be upon him) is repeatedly described in the Qur'an as a *dhakir* (one who reminds), emphasizing that guidance is not about inserting new beliefs but about helping others remember what is already latent within their being.

The Qur'anic journey of the nafs is thus not a mystical escape but a rational, neurobiological, and moral transformation. It is about understanding how our minds work, how we deceive ourselves, and how we can move closer to truth—not by abandoning reason, but by perfecting it.

Conclusion

The illusion of the self, as explained by neuroscience, does not contradict spiritual traditions—it clarifies and empowers them. The Qur'anic concept of nafs is not mysticism but a model of psychological development and self-regulation that aligns with cutting-edge cognitive science. By recognizing that the self is a construct, not a command, we can begin to dismantle harmful egocentric patterns and move toward the state of *nafs al-mutma'innah*—the tranquil self-aligned with Haqq.

In this light, Mansoor al-Hallaj's proclamation "Ana al-Haqq" (I am the Truth) may not be a mystical claim of divinity but a cognitive realization of the falsehood of the ego and the unity of conscious existence. Such a realization, when stripped of ego and interpreted scientifically, reflects not arrogance, but the highest humility: the dissolution of the illusion of "I" into the eternal reality of Haqq.

Chapter 9: Ego Dissolution and Brain States

"We will show them Our signs in the horizons and within themselves until it becomes clear to them that it is the Truth."

(Qur'an, 41:53)

The phenomenon of ego dissolution—experiencing the breakdown or complete loss of one's usual sense of self—is a compelling area of study at the intersection of neuroscience, psychology, and consciousness studies. In modern scientific discourse, ego dissolution has been associated with meditative practices, psychedelic experiences, and even trauma-induced altered states. This chapter explores the neurobiological and psychological mechanisms underlying ego dissolution and links these findings with the Quranic notion of the self (nafs), transformation, and transcendence of ego.

The Nature of Ego and Its Dissolution

The "ego" is generally understood in neuroscience and psychology as the part of the mind responsible for constructing the narrative identity of a person— "I am this," "I did that," "I want this." This narrative is tightly linked to the brain's Default Mode Network (DMN), which becomes active when we are engaged in self-referential thinking.

Ego dissolution refers to a temporary suppression or disintegration of this self-narrative. During this state, individuals often report feeling as if the boundary between self and world has vanished. These experiences are sometimes interpreted religiously as "merging with God" or metaphysically as experiencing "pure being."

However, a scientific examination reveals that these are altered brain states rather than supernatural events.

Meditation and Ego Dissolution

Research shows that long-term meditative practices can alter brain function and lead to ego-transcending states. In particular, mindfulness and non-dual awareness meditation techniques aim to shift attention away from self-referential processing.

- **Neurobiological Mechanisms:**
    - **Reduced DMN activity:** Studies using fMRI have shown that experienced meditators exhibit decreased activity in the medial prefrontal cortex (mPFC) and posterior cingulate cortex (PCC)—two central hubs of the DMN.
    - **Increased connectivity with attention networks:** As the DMN activity decreases, there is a rise in functional connectivity with attention and sensory networks, enhancing present-moment awareness.
- **Experiential Outcomes:**
    - Feelings of boundlessness and unity.
    - Reduced emotional reactivity.
    - A decrease in the salience of personal narrative or "ego."

These findings correlate with the Quranic call for self-purification and inward reflection, suggesting that consciousness can be refined to experience reality more clearly.

> "He has succeeded who purifies it [the self], and he has failed who corrupts it."
>
> (Qur'an 91:9-10)

Psychedelics and Ego Dissolution

Psychedelics like psilocybin (magic mushrooms), LSD, and DMT have also been shown to induce ego-dissolving states. While controversial, research in this field is providing profound insights into consciousness.

- **Scientific Studies:**
    - A 2016 study at Imperial College London found that high doses of psilocybin temporarily suppressed DMN activity and increased global brain connectivity.
    - Volunteers reported a "loss of the sense of self" and feelings of unity with the universe.
- **Implications:**
    - These experiences are not hallucinations but structured

perceptual alterations.
- ◦ The phenomenon parallels descriptions of 'Fanā' (annihilation of the ego) in Islamic tradition, but without any need for myth or miracle.

It's important to note that the Quran does not promote drug use, but the neurocognitive phenomena observed under psychedelics shed light on the mechanics of ego and self-awareness.

Trauma and Dissociative States

Extreme trauma can also result in altered states of consciousness. In some cases, individuals experience ego fragmentation or even ego dissolution as a coping mechanism.

- **Dissociation:** In cases of PTSD or extreme emotional shock, the brain may protect itself by "disconnecting" from the ego, leading to depersonalization or derealization.
- **Neurological Mechanism:** The prefrontal cortex becomes hypoactive while the amygdala (the fear center) becomes hyperactive.

Though this form of ego disruption is not spiritually enlightening, it provides a contrast: trauma can also break the ego, but without awareness or integration, it leads to psychological dysfunction rather than transformation.

Mystical States and Scientific Frameworks

Mystical experiences have been documented across cultures and traditions—from Christian mystics to Buddhist monks to Islamic Sufis. While their interpretations vary, the phenomenology is strikingly similar:

- Loss of the self
- Sense of unity with all things
- Timelessness
- Overwhelming awe and clarity

Science now considers these experiences a product of temporary changes in brain activity rather than supernatural encounters.

- **Neurotheology:** A growing field that studies how religious experiences correlate with brain activity. Researchers like Andrew Newberg have found that during mystical experiences, there is decreased activity in the orientation association area of the brain, leading to loss of boundary between self and other.

Quranic Perspective: Signs Within the Self

The Quran frequently calls upon human beings to reflect upon their own inner states to recognize truth.

> "And in your own selves—will you not then, see?"
> (Qur'an 51:21)

This call aligns with the modern scientific pursuit of understanding the mind. The Quran emphasizes that the self (nafs) is layered and must be purified and transcended to attain clarity and truth.

> "O tranquil self (nafs al-mutma'innah), return to your Lord, well-pleased and pleasing [to Him]."
>
> (Qur'an 89:27-28)

This suggests that the highest human goal is not to strengthen the ego, but to dissolve its illusions in pursuit of higher consciousness.

Conclusion

Ego dissolution is not a mystical fantasy but a neurocognitive reality. Whether through meditation, psychedelics, or altered brain states, the experience of losing the self has been documented, measured, and analyzed by modern science. The Quran, far from opposing these findings, supports the journey of self-purification, self-awareness, and eventual transcendence.

Mansoor al-Hallaj's declaration of "Ana al-Haqq" (I am the Truth) becomes clearer in this light: not a claim of divinity, but an experiential realization attained in a state where the ego is no longer the center of consciousness.

Ego dissolution, therefore, is not the end of the self but the beginning of awareness beyond it—a bridge between scientific understanding and Quranic insight.

In the next chapter, we will explore how Mansoor al-Hallaj's state can be interpreted not as madness or heresy, but as an advanced state of human consciousness understood by modern neuroscience and hinted at in sacred texts.

Chapter 10: Neuroscience Meets Ana al-Haqq

"We will show them Our signs in the horizons and within themselves until it becomes clear to them that it is the Truth (Al-Haqq)."

(Qur'an 41:53)

The proclamation of "Ana al-Haqq" (I am the Truth) by Mansoor al-Hallaj has been historically perceived as either a blasphemous declaration or a mystical utterance. However, with the advancements in neuroscience and a rational exploration of the concept of self and consciousness, we are now equipped to re-examine this statement through the scientific lens. This chapter draws parallels between modern findings in neuroscience—especially around ego dissolution and altered states of consciousness—and the psychological and philosophical condition from which "Ana al-Haqq" may have emerged.

Ego and Consciousness in the Human Brain

The human brain processes the concept of "self" largely through activity in the Default Mode Network (DMN), which includes the medial prefrontal cortex and posterior cingulate cortex. This network is active during introspective tasks and autobiographical memory recall, essentially when a person is "thinking about themselves."

When the DMN is suppressed—during meditation, deep prayer, psychedelic experiences, or mystical trances—individuals often report a loss of subjective self-awareness and describe a sensation of unity with something larger or eternal. This phenomenon, now called ego dissolution, has striking similarities to the mystical state that al-Hallaj might have experienced.

The Neuroscience of Ego Dissolution

Modern neuroscience has documented various brain states associated with ego dissolution. Functional MRI (fMRI) and EEG studies have revealed decreased activity in the DMN during such episodes, leading to a breakdown in the boundaries between self and environment. This is often accompanied by heightened connectivity in other areas of the brain, especially those associated with external sensory processing.

Studies by Dr. Robin Carhart-Harris and others at Imperial College London show that under the influence of psychedelics like psilocybin or LSD, brain scans indicate a collapse of ego boundaries. The self becomes "transparent," and the individual may feel unified with nature, consciousness, or an ultimate reality. The language used by these individuals parallels the essence of "Ana al-Haqq"—not as a delusional claim to divinity but as an experiential realization of the dissolution of the self into truth or reality.

"Ana al-Haqq" and the Dissolution of the Nafs

The Quran discusses various stages of the self (nafs):

- **Nafs al-Ammarah**: the commanding self—driven by base desires.
- **Nafs al-Lawwama**: the reproaching self—aware of moral responsibility.
- **Nafs al-Mutma'innah**: the tranquil self—at peace and in harmony with the divine order.

This transition from chaos to clarity is akin to ego dissolution. The Nafs al-Mutma'innah represents a state where the self ceases to resist the truth and instead submits entirely to it. From a neuroscientific perspective, this corresponds to a suppression of the DMN and a reduction in the egocentric worldview. Hallaj's statement, then, reflects not hubris, but transcendence: the self vanishes, and what remains is pure truth—Al-Haqq.

Neurobiological Evidence of Self-Transcendence

Neuroscience has identified several brain regions associated with self-awareness and transcendence:

- **Temporo-Parietal Junction (TPJ)**: involved in the distinction between self and others. Suppression here can lead to out-of-body experiences or unity states.
- **Insula**: processes interoceptive awareness (internal bodily states). Enhanced activity here is common in meditation and prayer.
- **Anterior Cingulate Cortex (ACC)**: associated with attention,

cognitive control, and error detection—often active during high-focus spiritual states.

When these regions are activated or deactivated in specific patterns, people report experiencing a "higher self," or even identifying with universal consciousness. This matches descriptions of Ana al-Haqq: an obliteration of the ego, and a fusion with what is perceived as the ultimate truth.

Behavior and Psychological Outcomes

One way to verify whether such states are pathological or transformative is to examine long-term behavior. In ego-dissolved individuals or those who have had mystical experiences, studies report:

- Increased altruism
- Reduced fear of death
- Enhanced psychological resilience
- Increased sense of unity with others and the environment
- Decreased egocentricity

These are precisely the traits historically attributed to mystics like al-Hallaj, who demonstrated self-sacrifice, spoke fearlessly, and rejected materialistic and dogmatic systems.

Consciousness and the Concept of Haqq

In the Qur'an, *Al-Haqq* is one of the defining attributes of the Creator. However, it is not defined as a personality or anthropomorphic being. It is the "Reality," the "Truth," the essence that underlies all existence:

> "That is because Allah is the Truth (al-Haqq), and that which they call upon besides Him is falsehood..."
>
> (Qur'an 22:62)

In neuroscience, consciousness is the substrate of all subjective experience. According to Integrated Information Theory (IIT) by Giulio Tononi, consciousness is a system's capacity to integrate information. Roger Penrose and Stuart Hameroff's Orchestrated Objective Reduction (Orch-OR) theory suggests consciousness might be a fundamental property of the universe, akin to gravity or space-time. If so, consciousness and *al-Haqq* share a domain—an eternal, underlying reality from which all emerges and returns.

When a highly conscious mind, free from ego and bias, proclaims "Ana al-Haqq," it is not elevating itself to God, but rather acknowledging the evaporation of the false self into the universal truth. Neuroscience validates this not as insanity but as a distinct mental and neural phenomenon.

Ana al-Haqq: An Epistemological Transformation

Rather than being a metaphysical claim, "Ana al-Haqq" can be seen as an epistemological shift—a change in how one knows, experiences, and relates to reality. In neuroscience, this parallels a state where sensory boundaries and categorical distinctions dissolve, allowing the brain to experience a non-dual state of awareness.

This resonates with the Qur'anic invitation to reflect on the signs within the self and the universe (41:53). It aligns with the realization that the constructed ego is an illusion and that beneath this illusion lies a deeper, more universal truth.

Conclusion

The intersection of neuroscience and the mystical statement "Ana al-Haqq" reveals profound insights. What was once condemned as heretical can now be re-interpreted as a scientifically observable state of consciousness. The declaration reflects not arrogance but a dissolution of ego, a return to reality as described in the Quran—Al-Haqq.

This chapter establishes that Hallaj's experience was not a mystical anomaly, but a neurocognitive transformation supported by scientific evidence. His statement marks the loss of individual identity and the emergence of universal consciousness. Through neuroscience, we now understand that such states are not delusions, but powerful transformations rooted in the biology of the human brain.

As we continue, the next chapter will explore how these neural states interact with language, perception, and spiritual metaphors, further bridging the gap between science and revelation.

Chapter 11: Quranic Insight into Human Mind and Perception

The Quran, unlike many religious texts, approaches the human mind not merely in terms of moral judgment or spiritual abstraction, but as a complex system of awareness, perception, cognition, and decision-making. Without resorting to speculative mysticism, the Quran identifies several distinct aspects of the human internal experience, such as *Qalb* (قلب), *Sadr* (صدر), and *Nafs* (نفس), which resonate with modern psychological and neuroscientific models of consciousness and cognition. This chapter aims to explore the Quranic depiction of the mind through these terms, offering a rational and scientifically grounded perspective.

Qalb: The Cognitive Heart of the Quran

In traditional interpretations, *Qalb* is often translated as "heart," but this literal translation fails to capture the term's contextual use in the Quran. The *Qalb* is described not as the anatomical organ but as a center of understanding, reflection, and intentionality. This function aligns more closely with the cognitive functions of the brain—specifically those regions associated with conscious awareness, decision-making, and emotional regulation.

Numerous Quranic verses support this cognitive view of *Qalb*:

> "They have hearts (*Qulub*) with which they do not understand..." (Quran 7:179)

This clearly indicates that *Qalb* is linked to comprehension, not mere emotionality. In modern neuroscience, similar functions are carried out by the prefrontal cortex, which is responsible for complex cognitive behavior, personality expression, and decision-making.

Furthermore, the Quran describes *Qalb* as the locus of guidance and deviation:

> "Allah has set a seal upon their hearts..." (Quran 2:7)

This verse implies that *Qalb* is malleable and influenced by conscious and subconscious factors. In neurological terms, this could relate to neural plasticity and how sustained behaviors and thoughts can reinforce or diminish certain neural pathways, shaping a person's moral and rational framework.

Sadr: The Emotional and Subconscious Space

صدر (*Sadr*), often translated as "chest" or "bosom," represents a deeper or more subconscious part of the self in Quranic terminology. It is frequently mentioned in contexts where inner emotions, intentions, or anxieties reside. For instance:

> "He knows what is within the *sudur* (plural of *sadr*)." (Quran 57:6)

This aspect of the psyche corresponds closely with what modern psychology describes as the subconscious mind. It is the part of the mind that stores automatic functions, emotional reactions, and deep-rooted beliefs. Neuroscientifically, *Sadr* may correlate with brain structures such as the limbic system, which governs emotions, memory processing, and instinctive responses.

Moreover, when the Quran speaks about constriction of the *Sadr*, it relates to psychological stress or cognitive dissonance:

> "We know that your *sadr* is constrained by what they say." (Quran 15:97)

This psychological response is mirrored in the activity of the anterior cingulate cortex and amygdala—regions of the brain activated during emotional pain, social exclusion, or conflict.

Nafs: The Self in Motion

Nafs (نفس) is perhaps the most comprehensive Quranic term for the self. Unlike *Qalb* and *Sadr*, which refer to specific faculties of perception and emotion, *Nafs* refers to the entire construct of the self, encompassing desire, awareness, moral conscience, and identity.

The Quran identifies different states or levels of *Nafs*, each corresponding to stages in personal development:

1. **Nafs al-Ammarah** (Commanding Self):

"Indeed, the *nafs* is ever-inclined to evil..." (Quran 12:53) This reflects the impulsive self—driven by primal desires and lacking self-regulation. This can be associated with the brain's reward system, including the basal ganglia and dopaminergic circuits.

1. **Nafs al-Lawwama** (Self-Reproaching Self):

"And I swear by the self-reproaching *nafs*..." (Quran 75:2) This is the self that has developed moral reflection but still struggles. Neuroscientific parallels can be found in regions involved in self-monitoring, such as the medial prefrontal cortex.

1. **Nafs al-Mutmainnah** (Tranquil Self):

"O tranquil *nafs*, return to your Lord..." (Quran 89:27-30) This stage represents cognitive maturity and emotional balance—where one is aligned with truth and inner peace. From a scientific perspective, this state would reflect an optimal integration of rational control (prefrontal cortex), emotional regulation (amygdala), and self-awareness (default mode network).

These three levels of *Nafs* do not signify different entities but evolving stages in the human psychological and ethical journey. They show how the Quran views personal development not as static but as a dynamic process requiring introspection, correction, and alignment with truth (*Haqq*).

Quranic Mind: A Model Without Superstition

The Quran does not describe the mind using mystical or esoteric language. It never promotes supernatural possession, trances, or mythical dualities. Rather, it identifies clear layers of the human cognitive-emotional system and discusses them in terms of understanding, awareness, moral choice, and accountability.

While classical Sufi literature often drifted into metaphorical or miraculous interpretations, the Quran remains grounded. It speaks directly to the human experience—addressing anger, fear, hope, anxiety, and self-deception—all through the lens of rational moral engagement.

Unlike later theological traditions, the Quran does not conflate spirituality with escape from reality. Rather, it invites individuals to deeply reflect on themselves:

> "And in yourselves, will you not then reflect?" (Quran 51:21)

This call to introspection is strikingly close to what neuroscience today encourages: self-awareness as a key to behavioral change and mental clarity.

The Mind as a Responsible Agent

The Quran repeatedly emphasizes that humans are accountable because they possess faculties of reasoning and awareness. These faculties are not external spirits or forces but internal capabilities endowed by creation.

> "He gave you hearing, sight, and *af'idah* (minds/hearts)." (Quran 16:78)

The word *af'idah* used here indicates centers of inner feeling and judgment, possibly equivalent to what we now call the affective and cognitive parts of the brain. The emphasis is on use: those who do not engage these faculties are likened to cattle or worse (Quran 7:179).

This makes the Quran's cognitive anthropology fully aligned with modern psychology: humans are morally responsible because they can know, reflect, and choose.

Conclusion: The Quranic Conscious Self

In the Quran, the human self is a multi-layered, evolving consciousness—comprised of *Qalb* (the rational and reflective mind), *Sadr* (the emotional and subconscious space), and *Nafs* (the overarching personal identity). These are not mystical constructs but deeply rational concepts that modern neuroscience can meaningfully interpret.

By grounding its model of the mind in functional and moral cognition, the Quran offers a timeless, logical, and non-superstitious understanding of the human condition. Its focus on introspection, moral development, and cognitive integrity aligns perfectly with what the scientific community now understands about the mind and consciousness.

Thus, the Quranic model of the human mind is not just spiritually profound—it is psychologically and neurologically precise. It offers a path of conscious evolution through awareness, emotional regulation, and ethical responsibility, free from the illusions of supernaturalism or fatalism.

Chapter 12: Is Haqq Within Us? Quran and Inner Reality

"And in yourselves, do you not see?" — Quran 51:21

The quest to understand the divine, or "Haqq" (Truth), has often led seekers both outward and inward. Among the Quran's profound calls for contemplation, verse 51:21— "And in yourselves, do you not see?"—stands as a striking invitation to self-exploration. This chapter examines the Quranic encouragement toward internal realization of truth and investigates whether "Haqq" is something discoverable within the human self. Through the lens of neuroscience and Quranic insight, we explore whether the divine truth is embedded not in abstract theology, but within the architecture of human consciousness.

1. What is Haqq? Revisiting the Concept

As previously discussed, the term "Haqq" in the Quran refers to an absolute, unchanging truth. It is not a figure, nor a mythological being, but rather the foundation of existence itself. It appears in many verses to refer to divine order, objective reality, justice, and the essential truth behind all creation. To claim that Haqq is within us does not mean that a person becomes God, but that the structure of human consciousness is innately aligned to discover this ultimate truth.

The Quran emphasizes that truth is not something external to the human condition. It invites reflection both in the natural world and within ourselves:

"We will show them Our signs in the horizons and within themselves until it becomes clear to them that it is the Truth." (Quran 41:53)

This verse places internal perception at par with external observation as a path to recognizing divine truth.

2. Consciousness: The Mirror of Haqq

Neuroscience defines consciousness as the ability to be aware of and to reflect upon one's experiences, perceptions, and identity. The Quran, too, places immense importance on perception, insight, and realization ("basirah"), indicating a type of internal light or cognitive awareness that can perceive truth.

In recent studies, consciousness has been shown to possess hierarchical layers—from basic awareness to meta-cognition, where the brain not only knows but knows that it knows. This depth of internal reflection is what sets human consciousness apart. The Quran echoes this in its repeated insistence on introspection, self-questioning, and awareness of inner states. These faculties are not accidental byproducts of evolution; rather, they are tools for discovering Haqq.

3. The Role of Qalb and Insight

The Quran uses the term "Qalb" (translated often as heart but better understood as the core or center of cognition) to describe the seat of understanding. Numerous verses associate Qalb with reasoning, reflection, and spiritual insight:

"They have hearts (Qulub) with which they do not understand..." (Quran 7:179)

This points to a cognitive dimension embedded within the self, which can either remain dormant or be activated through reflection. Haqq, being pure and absolute truth, resonates with the Qalb that is awake and attuned.

When the Qalb is corrupted, distracted, or veiled, the human being cannot perceive truth, despite having sensory and intellectual faculties. When it is purified and aligned, it becomes a mirror of Haqq.

4. The Brain as the Vehicle of Divine Perception

Neuroscientifically, the brain contains mechanisms for inner perception. The Default Mode Network (DMN), active during introspection, is essential for self-referential thought. Mindfulness practices, silence, and introspection reduce DMN activity, creating space for a non-egoic awareness that aligns with what many mystical traditions call "divine union."

In such states, the individual often reports feeling one with everything, experiencing timelessness, and realizing a form of truth beyond language or intellect. This state is scientifically explainable yet spiritually significant. These experiences are often accompanied by decreased activity in the ego-centric regions and increased activity in areas associated with compassion and unity.

Thus, when the Quran invites us to look within, it corresponds to what neuroscience now understands as the potential for consciousness to transcend the self and touch a deeper layer of reality—one that can be described as Haqq.

5. Human Fitrah and Alignment with Haqq

The Quran refers to "Fitrah"—the natural disposition upon which humans are created:

"So, direct your face toward the religion, inclining to truth. [Adhere to] the Fitrah of Allah upon which He has created [all] people." (Quran 30:30)

Fitrah implies that human beings are not born disconnected from truth, but rather inherently tuned to it. The Haqq is within us not in essence but in potential. The purpose of life, then, becomes the rediscovery of this alignment through purification (tazkiyah), self-awareness, and living justly.

Neuroscience supports this with findings that moral reasoning, empathy, and altruism are built into the neural architecture of the human brain. Even infants show signs of basic fairness and compassion, implying an innate moral compass.

6. Inner Signs and Self-Realization

The Quranic verse 51:21 is direct in its call:

"And in yourselves, do you not see?"

This is not merely a poetic metaphor; it is an ontological claim. It suggests that the journey to divine realization is not solely through dogma, ritual, or clerical authority, but through self-exploration, questioning, reflection, and inner refinement.

True belief, according to the Quran, is not blind imitation but comes after "yaqeen" (certainty), which is earned through evidence and reflection. Haqq must be experienced personally to be truly understood.

When the individual, through reflection, detaches from ego, false identity, and social conditioning, the truth within becomes clearer. This matches the state described in the Quran as "Nafs-e-Mutmainnah"—the self at peace—having realized its place in the larger scheme of existence.

7. Haqq as the Cognitive Destination

The ultimate goal of inner realization is not self-glorification but the annihilation of falsehood. The Quran states:

"Rather, we dash the truth (Haqq) upon falsehood, and it destroys it." (Quran 21:18)

The human being, in this framework, becomes a battlefield where falsehood (ego, delusion, social lies) is destroyed by truth (inner clarity, divine awareness). The destruction of the self's illusion is not a loss but a liberation.

Haqq, then, is not implanted like a gene but is the natural endpoint of conscious evolution. It is what remains when ignorance, illusion, and ego are removed.

8. Conclusion: Seeing the Divine Within

The Quran's consistent call to reflection and internal awareness is not philosophical speculation—it is a directive backed by neurological and psychological evidence. The capacity to perceive Haqq lies in the human being's cognitive, emotional, and moral faculties. It is through conscious refinement and sincere reflection that the self comes to mirror the divine truth.

"Ana al-Haqq"—if understood in this context—is not a claim of divinity but a realization that the deepest layer of the human experience is not isolated from truth. It is a recognition that when the self is purified and the mind is awake, it becomes a mirror in which the Haqq is reflected.

The Quran thus encourages not blind faith, but inner discovery. As chapter 51:21 asks: *"And in yourselves, do you not see?"*—the answer lies in our willingness to look.

Chapter 13: Prophetic Consciousness and Revelation

"It is not but a revelation revealed. Taught to him by one intense in strength."
— Quran, Surah An-Najm (53:4-5)

Throughout history, the phenomenon of revelation has captivated scholars, philosophers, theologians, and neuroscientists alike. In Islamic discourse, a *Nabi* (prophet) is not a magician, mystic, or mere visionary, but a conscious, rational, and fully self-aware human being who operates at the pinnacle of cognitive clarity and moral insight. This chapter explores the concept of prophetic consciousness in the Quranic context and investigates its intersection with modern neuroscience. By logically interpreting prophetic revelation, we distinguish the conscious states of a true *Nabi* from hallucinations, psychotic episodes, or emotionally driven intuition. Our aim is to establish that the Quranic revelation is a product of a heightened state of consciousness, not a violation of natural laws.

The Nature of Revelation (Wahi) in the Quran

The Quran consistently refers to revelation (*Wahi*) as a structured communication. It is not mystical or irrational. It is described as a deliberate and intelligible process where truth is conveyed to the prophet in a way that aligns with understanding and contemplation. The term *Wahi* itself, in Arabic, does not necessarily imply supernaturalism. It means a focused, subtle form of inspiration—whether through thoughts, dreams, signs, or direct communication.

Consider these verses:

> "Indeed, We have revealed to you as We revealed to Noah and the prophets after him." (Quran 4:163)

> "We do not send the messengers except as bringers of good tidings and warners." (Quran 6:48)

This shows that revelation is part of a continuum of human intellectual development. The *Nabi* is chosen because he can process, articulate, and embody this truth in a socially transformative manner.

Who is a Nabi? A Model of High Cognitive and Moral Awareness

In Quranic context, a *Nabi* is someone with exceptional self-mastery, moral integrity, and cognitive sophistication. The Quran does not describe prophets as beings with magical powers or mystical ecstasies. Instead, they are described with terms like:

- **Hakeem (wise)**
- **Sadiq (truthful)**
- **Sabir (patient)**
- **Mutawakkil (trusting in process and cause-effect)**

The defining feature of a prophet is their ability to perceive reality beyond ego, prejudice, and social delusion. This perception enables them to speak a higher truth (*Haqq*), often in defiance of prevailing customs and power structures.

States of Consciousness in Neuroscience

In neuroscience, consciousness is broadly understood as the ability to be aware of oneself and the environment. Advanced levels of consciousness involve:

- **Metacognition** – the ability to reflect on one's thoughts
- **Self-regulation** – conscious control over impulses and emotions
- **Empathy and ethical reasoning** – understanding others and moral consequences

Neuroimaging studies of meditators, philosophers, and highly reflective individuals show increased activity in regions like the **prefrontal cortex**, which is responsible for moral reasoning and long-term planning. Prophetic consciousness, as described in the Quran, aligns with this upper spectrum of integrated awareness.

Prophetic Revelation vs. Madness

Many critics have historically equated revelation with hallucination or psychosis. But there are critical distinctions:

1. **Clarity vs. Confusion:** Prophets speak with clarity and structure. They present consistent moral and social frameworks. In contrast, psychosis involves disorganized thoughts and delusional content.
2. **Responsibility vs. Delusion:** Prophets demonstrate responsibility, empathy, and future vision. They reform societies. Psychotic episodes often lack accountability.
3. **Moral Consistency vs. Fragmentation:** Quranic revelation upholds a unified moral vision, whereas hallucinations often lead to erratic, self-destructive behavior.

Prophets face inner and outer resistance, but their message is anchored in logic, ethics, and profound social insight. The Quran repeatedly challenges listeners to "reflect," "use reason," and "see signs." These are not characteristics of delusional content—they are appeals to conscious engagement.

Inspiration and Prophetic Consciousness

The Quran refers to *Ilham* (inspiration) and *Wahi* (structured revelation) as distinct. For example:

> "And We inspired the mother of Moses..." (Quran 28:7)

This is different from the structured message given to prophets, but it indicates that inspiration operates on a spectrum. All humans can access intuitive insight, but only those with disciplined awareness can sustain and articulate revelation. In neuroscience, this resembles the difference between a momentary insight and a sustained state of high-functioning awareness.

Prophetic Integrity and Social Responsibility

A hallmark of the prophetic mind is the ability to transcend personal gain. Prophets are not driven by reward, fame, or fear. They operate from a core of ethical responsibility. This is reflected in multiple Quranic verses:

> "Say, I do not ask you for any reward." (Quran 6:90)

This detachment from reward-seeking behavior is a sign of deep conscious control over ego-driven impulses. Modern neuroscience understands such detachment as an indication of executive function maturity—the ability to delay gratification for long-term purpose.

Prophets as Educators of Consciousness

The Quran presents prophets as **teachers**—those who liberate minds from falsehood. The verses repeatedly emphasize the role of reason, clarity, and moral awakening:

> "He is the one who sent among the unlettered a messenger...to teach them the Book and wisdom." (Quran 62:2)

They do not demand blind belief but invite reflective realization. This is the essence of high consciousness: to align inner clarity with social truth.

The Transformational Impact of Revelation

One of the most compelling evidences of prophetic consciousness is the transformation it causes—not only within the individual but within entire civilizations. Prophet Muhammad's message reformed the tribal, polytheistic, and unjust social structure of Arabia into a society governed by justice, rights, and knowledge. This kind of systemic transformation is impossible through hallucinations or delusions.

Wisdom versus Madness: Key Differences

Let us clarify how prophetic wisdom differs from both inspiration and mental illness:

- **Inspiration** is momentary and unstructured.
- **Madness** is delusional, inconsistent, and self-centered.
- **Prophetic consciousness** is structured, consistent, socially transformative, and logically defensible.

Revelation is not received through passive surrender but through the highest moral and rational engagement. It requires not only neurological capacity but also ethical maturity.

Conclusion: Prophethood as Conscious Evolution

The Quran never asks us to accept a prophet's claim blindly. It presents the *Nabi* as a rational being, deeply connected to truth (*Haqq*), who invites others into this elevated state of awareness. Prophethood, then, is not an exception to human nature—it is its most refined expression. The *Nabi* embodies what every human mind could aspire to become: fully awake, morally upright, and rationally grounded.

In this light, prophetic consciousness is the peak of human evolution—not in a biological sense, but in terms of awareness, responsibility, and clarity. The revelation they receive is not magic—it is insight, cultivated at the deepest level of being.

The Quran reminds us:

> "Indeed, this is a reminder for whoever has a heart or listens while he is present in mind." (Quran 50:37)

This verse signifies that revelation speaks to those capable of real listening—with the heart (Qalb), not just the ears. It is a message decoded only by a consciousness refined enough to receive it.

Chapter 14: Ana al-Haqq is not Blasphemy: A Scientific Defense

"We will show them Our signs in the horizons and within themselves until it becomes clear to them that it is the Truth." (Qur'an 41:53)

Introduction

The phrase "Ana al-Haqq" uttered by Mansoor Al-Hallaj has long been misinterpreted as a blasphemous statement by the religious orthodoxy. Translated as "I am the Truth," and considering that "Al-Haqq" is one of the attributes used for the Divine in the Qur'an, critics accused Hallaj of claiming divinity. However, when examined through the dual lenses of neuroscience and the Qur'an, the statement aligns not with heresy but with a scientifically valid and spiritually coherent concept: the loss of ego and the realization of the interconnected unity of consciousness.

This chapter aims to defend the statement logically, scientifically, and quranically—dissecting what Hallaj may have truly meant, and how the religious interpretation failed to understand the nature of consciousness and self.

Ana al-Haqq: Context and Meaning

The phrase "Ana al-Haqq" is not an isolated utterance but part of a larger mystical experience. Hallaj, as historical accounts suggest, entered a state of profound self-transcendence, wherein his sense of individual identity was annihilated. This phenomenon is now well-documented in neuroscience as ego dissolution.

From a Qur'anic perspective, the realization of one's inherent connection to Haqq (Truth) is not only permitted but encouraged. The Qur'an says:

> "And in yourselves, do you not see?" (Qur'an 51:21)

This verse urges self-reflection, suggesting that the truth (Haqq) is discoverable within human consciousness itself. Hallaj's experience of "I am the Truth" could be interpreted as the culmination of this internal exploration.

Neuroscience and the Disappearance of the Ego

Modern neuroscience has extensively studied the phenomenon of ego death. When the Default Mode Network (DMN) of the brain—responsible for the continuous sense of a separate self—is suppressed (through meditation, deep trauma, or psychedelics), subjects report feeling united with the universe, or with an abstract 'Truth.'

This state often leads to statements that mirror Hallaj's utterance. Patients under the influence of psilocybin, for instance, report: "I became one with the universe," or "I merged with the source of all being."

These experiences are not delusional. They are repeatable, measurable, and consistent across cultures. What Hallaj experienced was likely a non-pathological, deeply altered state of consciousness where the boundaries between self and Truth dissolved.

Qur'anic Harmony with Self-Realization

The Qur'an does not advocate for a dualistic divide between man and God that makes any merging of truth and consciousness blasphemous. Instead, the text frequently points toward inner discovery and self-purification as paths to truth.

> "Successful indeed is the one who purifies it [the soul/self], and failed is the one who corrupts it." (Qur'an 91:9–10)

This purification is the process of stripping away the nafs al-ammarah (commanding self) to reach a state of mutma'innah (tranquil self). In this purified state, human consciousness aligns with divine will—not in essence, but in function.

Thus, when Hallaj said "Ana al-Haqq," he was not claiming to be God in essence. He was expressing a state where his individual ego no longer stood between himself and Truth.

Linguistic Fallacy of Blasphemy Accusation

Blasphemy, by definition, involves mocking or demeaning the Divine. However, Hallaj's statement did not mock, but rather, revered the Divine to such a degree that the self was obliterated in its presence. The statement "Ana al-Haqq" is linguistically a declaration of unity, not superiority.

From the standpoint of Arabic syntax, "Ana al-Haqq" uses a definite article "Al" (the), suggesting not personal ownership but identification with a universal principle. In Islamic metaphysics, Allah is not anthropomorphized but described through attributes—Haqq being one of them. If consciousness realizes its inseparable existence from these attributes, declaring "Ana al-Haqq" could be seen as expressing alignment, not usurpation.

The Role of Fear and Power in Religious Misinterpretation

It is crucial to examine why such statements are branded as heretical. Often, it is not theology but politics and power structures that fuel such accusations. When individuals like Hallaj articulate spiritual ideas that decentralize religious authority, they become threats to institutional power.

The religious class, lacking understanding of consciousness or neuroscience, had only two tools: accusation and execution. This behavior echoes the Qur'anic critique of those who suppress truth for fear of losing authority:

> "And when it is said to them, 'Follow what Allah has revealed,' they say, 'Rather, we will follow what we found our fathers doing.'" (Qur'an 2:170)

This traditionalism resists new realizations even when they align with divine revelation.

The Scientific Model of Unity Consciousness

Science today proposes models such as Integrated Information Theory (IIT) and Orchestrated Objective Reduction (Orch-OR) which suggest that consciousness is not confined to individuals but may be a fundamental aspect of reality. In such models, the feeling of being a separate self is a byproduct of brain processes, and consciousness itself may be an interconnected field.

This view echoes Hallaj's spiritual realization. When he said "Ana al-Haqq," he might have been articulating a moment when his individual identity collapsed into this universal field of consciousness—the 'Haqq'.

The Prophet Muhammad and the Idea of Truth

Even the Prophet Muhammad, according to Qur'anic description, experienced an ego-transcending mission. The Qur'an states:

> "You did not throw when you threw, but Allah threw." (Qur'an 8:17)

This verse demonstrates that the Prophet's will was aligned so entirely with the divine that his actions were expressions of divine will. If such a model is accepted for prophets, Hallaj's statement—coming from a lesser but similar experience—should not be interpreted as blasphemy but as a recognition of a state wherein personal ego dissolves in truth.

Hallaj's Execution: A Reflection of Human Ignorance

The punishment of Hallaj represents not the victory of theology but the failure of reason. In light of both Qur'anic insight and modern science, the condemnation appears tragically misplaced.

> "And thus, We have made for every prophet an enemy among the criminals. But sufficient is your Lord as a guide and a helper." (Qur'an 25:31)

The opposition to Hallaj mirrors this verse. His spiritual awakening threatened the existing structure, and so he was labeled a criminal rather than a seeker of Haqq.

Conclusion: The Scientific Vindication of Ana al-Haqq

Through neuroscience, we now understand that human consciousness is capable of experiences where ego boundaries dissolve and a universal reality is perceived. Through the Qur'an, we see that the pursuit of inner truth, the purification of the self, and the alignment with divine principles is not heretical but divinely ordained.

Thus, "Ana al-Haqq" must be reinterpreted—not as a declaration of divinity, but as a scientifically and theologically defensible articulation of a moment where self and truth were not separate. This interpretation does not blaspheme the Divine; it reveals the depth of human potential to perceive it.

Mansoor Al-Hallaj's words, once feared, now find validation in both the lab and the scripture. The truth he proclaimed was not about himself, but about what lies at the deepest core of us all—Haqq.

Chapter 15: Modern Neuroscience Supports the Ana al-Haqq State

"We will show them Our signs in the horizons and within themselves until it becomes clear to them that it is the Truth." (Quran 41:53)

The mystical utterance "Ana al-Haqq" (I am the Truth), famously declared by Mansoor Al-Hallaj, has long been a subject of debate, reverence, and controversy. While traditionally approached through religious or philosophical frameworks, contemporary neuroscience opens a new and fascinating avenue of inquiry. This chapter explores how the latest findings in neuroscience support the experiential basis of Al-Hallaj's state, stripping away superstitions and mystical embellishments, and presenting a scientific explanation for such elevated states of consciousness. The goal is not to mystify the phenomenon but to logically examine how the brain may experience and interpret what Al-Hallaj described.

The Brain and the Self: Breaking the Illusion

One of the fundamental insights of neuroscience over the past few decades is the discovery that the sense of a fixed, separate "self" is an illusion generated by the brain. The Default Mode Network (DMN), a set of interconnected brain regions including the medial prefrontal cortex and posterior cingulate cortex, is central to our sense of self and autobiographical memory. Disruptions in the DMN, particularly through practices such as deep meditation or the controlled use of psychedelics, result in a diminished sense of ego and a greater feeling of unity with the environment, or what mystics have described as the 'One.'

This is relevant to "Ana al-Haqq" because Al-Hallaj's statement can be interpreted as arising from such a neurocognitive state, where the boundaries between the ego and a universal reality dissolve. The result is not a delusional identity with God, but an experience of self as integrated into the totality of existence—which in the Quran is repeatedly described as "al-Haqq."

Ego Dissolution: The Scientific Correlate of Fanā

Fanā (self-annihilation) is a concept closely related to ego dissolution, and neuroscience now offers empirical evidence to support the reality of such states. Functional MRI (fMRI) scans show that during ego-dissolving experiences, the DMN becomes less active, while areas of the brain associated with sensory integration and present awareness (like the insular cortex and parietal lobes) become more active. This realignment of brain function corresponds with feelings of unity, loss of personal identity, and deep peace—all of which are described in mystical traditions as signs of merging with the Divine.

When Hallaj said "Ana al-Haqq," he might have been describing a state where the self, as a mental construct, had fully dissolved, leaving only pure awareness—an experience that modern neuroscience increasingly understands and can measure.

Consciousness as a Universal Field

Some leading theories in consciousness studies suggest that consciousness may not be merely an emergent property of brain activity but a fundamental aspect of reality. Integrated Information Theory (IIT), proposed by Giulio Tononi, suggests that consciousness arises from the integration of information across a system. Roger Penrose and Stuart Hameroff's Orch-OR theory goes further to postulate that consciousness arises at the quantum level within microtubules in neurons.

While these theories are still debated, they are part of a serious scientific effort to understand consciousness beyond simple material interactions. They resonate deeply with Quranic language, which does not treat consciousness as confined to humans but as something that permeates existence ("Everything glorifies Him, but you do not understand their glorification." — Quran 17:44).

If consciousness is indeed more fundamental and not localized in the individual brain, then Hallaj's statement could reflect an experience of tuning into this universal consciousness, perceived through the lens of Arabic and Quranic vocabulary as "Haqq."

The Neuroscience of Mystical Experiences

Recent studies on mystical experiences have documented changes in the brain that correspond with what spiritual practitioners describe. For example:

- **Mystical unity experiences** are associated with decreased activity in the DMN and increased connectivity between brain regions not usually in communication.
- **Feelings of boundlessness or oneness** have been correlated with the neurotransmitter serotonin and specific receptor sites (5-HT2A).
- **Studies at institutions like Johns Hopkins University and Imperial College London** have found that controlled administration of substances like psilocybin can reliably induce ego dissolution, deep spiritual insight, and profound peace.

These results are not endorsing drug use but demonstrate that the brain is capable of producing states consistent with what mystics like Hallaj have described. More importantly, they point to an underlying structure in the human brain that allows for the experience of transcending the personal ego.

Neurotheology: A New Approach Without Superstition

Neurotheology is an emerging field that studies the relationship between brain function and spiritual experience. It does not affirm or deny the existence of God but examines how religious and transcendent experiences manifest in the brain. Andrew Newberg's work in this field shows that during deep prayer or meditation, the parietal lobes (which help us orient in space and define boundaries of the self) become less active. This corresponds with experiences of boundlessness and unity often described in mystical states.

These are precisely the types of experiences that Hallaj would have had when he uttered "Ana al-Haqq." Rather than being signs of delusion or heresy, these states represent a real and measurable alteration in brain function that aligns with centuries of spiritual insight.

Quranic Alignment with Scientific Discovery

The Quran repeatedly draws attention to the human mind and invites reflection and introspection:

- "And in yourselves, do you not see?" (Quran 51:21)
- "We created man and know what his soul whispers to him, and We are closer to him than his jugular vein." (Quran 50:16)

These verses are not mystical in the sense of irrationality. Rather, they are deeply rational prompts toward self-awareness. If Al-Haqq is experienced when the self becomes quiet and perceptive, then these Quranic verses align perfectly with modern cognitive neuroscience, which tells us that insight, awareness, and peace emerge when the ego is silenced.

The Quran does not encourage hallucination or irrationality. Instead, it asks humans to use their intellect ('aql), to reflect (tafakkur), and to recognize inner and outer realities. This cognitive process, when it reaches the highest maturity, may mirror the very state of awareness described by Al-Hallaj in his final moments of unity.

Moving Beyond Superstition

One of the greatest obstacles to understanding mystical statements like "Ana al-Haqq" is the cultural weight of miracle-based narratives and superstitions that emerged centuries after the original teachings. Hallaj was later transformed into a saint surrounded by mythical stories of resurrection, levitation, and divine favor. But none of this is required to explain his core insight.

From a neuroscience perspective, what Hallaj experienced was not supernatural—it was superconscious. It was a form of perception made available by the natural architecture of the human brain, particularly when the ego or self-referential circuits are diminished.

Rejecting these superstitions is not a denial of the beauty or power of Hallaj's experience. It is a return to its purity. It is an invitation to understand the state of "Ana al-Haqq" as a pinnacle of human awareness, accessible through disciplined mental focus, ethical clarity, and deep cognitive refinement.

Conclusion

Modern neuroscience, in its study of consciousness, ego, and mystical experience, provides a profound and rational framework for understanding Mansoor Al-Hallaj's declaration "Ana al-Haqq." Far from being heretical or irrational, this utterance represents an advanced psychological and cognitive state wherein the illusion of separation fades, and the individual experiences alignment with what the Quran calls "Haqq"—The Absolute Reality.

In moving beyond myth and into scientific insight, we honor the essence of Hallaj's experience and make it accessible to modern seekers—not through rituals and miracles, but through deep inner exploration, verified by empirical understanding.

The state of "Ana al-Haqq" is not the domain of saints or prophets alone. It is a latent potential of the human mind, validated by science, anticipated by the Quran, and realized by those who dare to dissolve the illusion of self.

Chapter 16: Consciousness, Creator, and the Quran

Unifying Consciousness as 'Haqq'

The phrase "Ana al-Haqq" (I am the Truth) spoken by Mansur al-Hallaj ignited centuries of debate. But the deeper significance of this statement can only be understood when we analyze the unifying concept of *Haqq* (Truth) in relation to consciousness and the Quranic worldview. In this chapter, we explore whether the Quran implies the universe is underpinned by a unifying, infinite consciousness — a being or essence that is not anthropomorphic, but the very structure of reality. This aligns with the philosophical and scientific notion of a conscious cosmos, and places the idea of 'Haqq' at the center of existence.

The Quran, when read without traditional theological filters, presents *Haqq* not as a personified deity, but as the ultimate, inescapable reality. This resonates profoundly with the modern philosophical and neuroscientific understanding of consciousness: an unobservable yet omnipresent phenomenon that underpins thought, awareness, and identity.

Quranic Language of Consciousness

The Quran repeatedly uses terms such as *Qalb* (mind/inner consciousness), *Sadr* (mental openness), *Nafs* (self), and *Ruh* (spirit or breath of awareness). The semantic structure of these terms consistently points toward a graded model of human consciousness, where internal awareness is a direct channel to perceiving divine reality.

In Quran 51:21, we find the verse: "And in yourselves, do you not see?" This rhetorical question is a call to self-reflection, not merely physical but cognitive and conscious. The Quran asserts that the signs of truth and divine presence are not just in the world around us (*afaq*) but within the depths of our own consciousness (*anfus*). This provides a clear ontological bridge between the self and the ultimate reality — *Haqq*.

Moreover, the Quran never demands blind faith. Instead, it calls repeatedly to *taaqiloon* (those who reason), *yatafakkaroon* (those who reflect), and *yash'uroon* (those who are aware). These appeals directly involve faculties of higher consciousness. The implication is profound: the human being is not merely a biological entity, but a vessel capable of directly interfacing with the structure of the cosmos through awareness.

Haqq as an Abstract, Infinite Consciousness

Contrary to popular theological interpretations, the Quran does not reduce *Haqq* to a being with human-like traits. Nowhere does the Quran state that God is a man, nor does it assign a name like "Father" or anthropomorphic image. Instead, *Allah* is described through attributes (e.g., *Al-Hayy* – the Living, *Al-'Aleem* – the All-Knowing, *An-Nur* – the Light) that point toward functions or states of awareness rather than physical form. These names are metaphors or qualities — and as previously discussed, the enumeration of the 99 names is a post-Quranic development from Hadith literature, not a Quranic prescription.

In this regard, *Haqq* (Truth) is the most foundational attribute because it does not denote a role, an emotion, or a temporal act. It denotes pure, objective, unchanging reality. When Al-Hallaj said "Ana al-Haqq," he was not claiming to be God in a monotheistic sense, but rather expressing his annihilation of ego and absorption into the only constant reality — that which is always true.

This interpretation aligns well with neuroscience and philosophy of consciousness. As thinkers like David Chalmers have argued, consciousness is not reducible to physical processes. It may instead be a fundamental feature of the universe, akin to space-time or gravity. The Quran appears to anticipate this view by suggesting that *Haqq* (the ultimate truth) is the underlying reality, and everything else is a projection, a *zann* (guess or illusion), or *batil* (falsehood).

The Self, the Veil, and the Real

Surah Al-Baqarah (2:7) describes how the hearts (Qulub) of some people are sealed, their hearing dulled, and their sight veiled. This metaphor is not about punishment alone, but a description of psychological states. People are unaware not because the truth is absent, but because consciousness is obstructed. In contrast, those who are spiritually awakened — those whose *Qalb* is open — are able to perceive the signs of *Haqq* everywhere.

From a neuroscientific standpoint, this maps well with the concept of *Default Mode Network* (DMN) in the brain, which creates the illusion of self. When the DMN is quieted — such as in meditation or through psychedelics — individuals report ego dissolution and a sense of oneness with a larger, timeless presence. These experiences mirror descriptions found in the Quran of *Nafs al-Mutmainnah* (the content self), which returns to its source in peace.

Hence, the Quranic idea of returning to Allah, as stated in 89:27-30 — "O tranquil soul, return to your Lord, well-pleased and pleasing (to Him)" — does not suggest physical movement but the dissolution of the illusion of separateness. The 'return' is psychological and existential: a merging into the conscious field that underlies all things — *Haqq*.

Scientific Frameworks of Conscious Cosmos

Modern science increasingly entertains the possibility that consciousness is not an emergent property but a fundamental one. Integrated Information Theory (IIT), proposed by Giulio Tononi, posits that consciousness arises from the integration of information. Under this theory, any system that integrates information has some level of consciousness. This perspective is not confined to brains but extends to the universe itself.

Similarly, physicist Roger Penrose and anesthesiologist Stuart Hameroff proposed the Orchestrated Objective Reduction (Orch-OR) theory, suggesting that consciousness arises from quantum processes within neurons, and possibly beyond. These theories are speculative, yet they converge on one implication: consciousness may be woven into the very fabric of reality.

If this is the case, then the Quran's repeated assertion that everything glorifies Allah (Quran 17:44) becomes profoundly meaningful. "The seven heavens and the earth and whatever is in them exalt Him. And there is not a thing except that it exalts [Allah] by His praise, but you do not understand their glorification." This could be read not as literal speech by inanimate objects, but as the expression of a conscious substrate that permeates all matter.

Unity of Consciousness and the Quranic Cosmos

The Quran frequently calls attention to the unity of all things. Surah Al-Ikhlas (112:1-4) states: "Say: He is Allah, One. Allah, the Eternal Refuge. He neither begets nor is born, nor is there to Him any equivalent."

This does not describe a biological entity or a tribal god. It points to an infinite, non-dual reality that is self-sufficient and beyond comparison. This matches the metaphysical idea that all distinctions — self/other, time/space, subject/object — are products of limited perception, not fundamental truths.

Consciousness, when elevated, dissolves these distinctions. This dissolution is not nihilistic but affirmative. As the false layers fall away, what remains is

Haqq — the truth that was always present, hidden behind the veil of the ego, culture, and illusion.

Ana al-Haqq Revisited: Not Heresy, but Discovery

When Hallaj said, "Ana al-Haqq," he was not elevating himself. He was negating his individual ego and affirming his dissolution into the unified consciousness that the Quran names *Haqq*. From a Quranic and neuroscientific perspective, this is not blasphemy but realization.

The Quran does not condemn introspection, reflection, or the exploration of consciousness. Instead, it frames these pursuits as noble. It is only when ego corrupts the mind, when *nafs al-ammarah* (commanding self) dominates, that one loses connection to truth. Hallaj, through deep introspection and what modern terms would call ego dissolution, experienced a state where only *Haqq* remained — and in that state, to say "I am Haqq" is not to claim divinity but to erase selfhood.

Conclusion: The Conscious Cosmos and the Quranic Vision

In conclusion, the Quranic portrayal of *Haqq* aligns remarkably with the idea of a conscious, unified field that underpins all existence. The concepts of *Qalb*, *Ruh*, *Nafs*, and *Sadr* form a multi-dimensional model of human consciousness. These are not metaphysical ornaments but scientifically plausible descriptions of human cognitive architecture.

The claim that "Ana al-Haqq" is heretical collapses under logical and neurological scrutiny. The Quran invites humanity to explore the inner and outer cosmos, and to witness the signs of truth — not as metaphors but as pathways to the ultimate reality. This reality is not a distant sky-God but the very fabric of being, the consciousness that breathes through all existence.

Thus, in both Quranic language and scientific logic, we are not separate from *Haqq*. We are immersed in it. The illusion is separateness; the truth is unity. The quest is not to ascend to divinity but to awaken to what already is: *Haqq*, the Absolute Consciousness.

Chapter 17: A New Understanding of Hallaj

"And say: The truth has come, and falsehood has vanished. Indeed, falsehood is bound to vanish." — Quran 17:81

The historical figure of Mansur al-Hallaj has long remained a subject of awe, fear, admiration, and controversy. His declaration *Ana al-Haqq* — "I am the Truth" — led to his brutal execution, yet the meaning behind his words has echoed through centuries. This book has attempted to separate myth from meaning, spirituality from superstition, and faith from fabricated tradition. It has sought to interpret Hallaj's phrase within the frameworks of modern neuroscience, the Quranic view of the self, and the universal quest for consciousness.

This final chapter offers a conclusive synthesis of the key insights presented in this work. It recasts Hallaj's phrase not as blasphemy or mysticism but as a profound psychological and spiritual truth: that the self, when purified of ego and illusion, becomes aware of its oneness with universal truth — *Haqq*.

Summary of Key Findings

1. Linguistic and Quranic Foundation of Haqq

The Quranic term *Haqq* does not refer to any individual but to an absolute, universal, objective reality — the source and end of all existence. Multiple verses affirm that Allah is *Al-Haqq* — the Truth — and that truth is embedded not only in the cosmos but also in the human self (Quran 51:21). The term *Ana al-Haqq*, when isolated from its historical and linguistic roots, appears to claim divinity. But when understood in the light of the Quran's own view of the self and consciousness, it can be interpreted as a reflection of deep unity with truth, not a claim to divinity.

2. The Illusion of the Self and the Role of Consciousness

Modern neuroscience reveals that our sense of "I" or self is not a fixed entity but a construct generated by specific brain networks, particularly the Default Mode Network (DMN). This network is responsible for generating internal narratives, identity, and ego. When this network is quieted — during deep meditation, mystical states, or near-death experiences — individuals report a state of ego dissolution and unity with a greater whole. Hallaj's statement is remarkably parallel to such states. It is not a declaration of deity but a testament of transcendence.

3. Quranic Psychology: Qalb, Nafs, and Sadr

The Quran outlines a multi-dimensional structure of human cognition. The *Qalb* (center of consciousness), *Sadr* (mental state or subconscious), and *Nafs* (self) are distinct but interconnected aspects of human perception. The Quran consistently calls for the purification of the *Nafs* and the illumination of the *Qalb*, describing stages of the self: *Nafs-e-Ammarah* (compulsive self), *Lawwamah* (self-reproaching), and *Mutmainnah* (content, harmonized). Hallaj's phrase corresponds to the final stage of *Mutmainnah*, where the self becomes so attuned to truth that its separateness dissolves.

4. The Prophet as a Model of Higher Consciousness

Prophets in the Quran are not magicians or miracle-workers; they are highly developed consciousnesses, aware of deeper layers of reality. Revelation is described not as auditory hallucination but as a process where the *Ruh* (spirit/consciousness) inspires the *Qalb* of the Prophet. Hallaj, though not a prophet, may be seen as a human who reached a heightened state of inner awareness where he perceived truth directly — an idea not inconsistent with Quranic descriptions.

5. Scientific Evidence for Ego Death

Studies in neuroscience and psychology now document ego-dissolving states through fMRI, EEG scans, and phenomenological interviews. Whether induced through meditation, psychedelic substances, trauma, or spontaneous mystical experiences, individuals in such states report a feeling of unity with everything, often expressed in language similar to Hallaj's. Crucially, these individuals do not exhibit pathological delusions but often emerge more compassionate, grounded, and aware. This aligns with the ethical and moral clarity evident in Hallaj's life and teachings.

A Scientific and Quranic Revival of Ana al-Haqq

We now stand at the confluence of two streams of thought: ancient spiritual wisdom and modern scientific understanding. Neuroscience provides empirical evidence of altered states of consciousness where ego is dissolved, and a universal awareness is perceived. The Quran, when interpreted free of tradition-bound limitations, confirms the inner journey toward truth and invites humanity to reflect inwardly. Together, they offer a bridge to reinterpret *Ana al-Haqq* not as an offense against God but as a discovery of God within.

This is not pantheism. It is not claiming that the self *is* God in a literal sense. Rather, it is an acknowledgment that the purified self perceives no separation between itself and the divine truth that animates the cosmos. As the Quran says:

> "We are closer to him than his jugular vein" — (Quran 50:16)

The proximity here is not spatial but existential. When one becomes fully aware, shedding layers of constructed ego, language may fail — but the heart (*Qalb*) may utter what the tongue fears: *Ana al-Haqq*.

Refuting Misuse and Superstition

While Sufi traditions have preserved many valuable insights, they also often cloaked them in metaphor, miracle-tales, and inaccessible language. Hallaj became both a symbol of enlightenment and a tool of mystification. His experience was co-opted by cults of personality and miracle-based narratives that turned inward realization into religious performance.

This book rejects such mythologizing. Hallaj's insight can be understood without invoking supernaturalism. It is neither a miracle nor heresy — it is a psychological transformation backed by emerging scientific models and rooted in Quranic consciousness.

A Warning from History

Hallaj's execution also offers a lesson: societies that suppress inner inquiry and critical reflection in the name of orthodoxy stagnate. Hallaj was not crucified for being mad — he was crucified for being too sane in a world that worshipped conformity. His death was not just a theological statement but a political act meant to control narrative, dogma, and collective psychology.

Toward a New Future of Religious Thought

The synthesis offered in this work advocates a reformation of spiritual inquiry. Religious truths must not be shielded from scientific validation. The Quran does not fear reason — it invites it. The message of *Ana al-Haqq* is not limited to a mystic but extends to anyone willing to confront the illusions of ego and awaken to inner truth. This is not a call to worship the self but to transcend it.

In this new light, Hallaj becomes not a martyr for blasphemy but a pioneer of human consciousness — a man who saw what others feared to see. And in seeing it, he spoke the unspeakable.

> *"He who knows himself, knows his Lord."* — (Prophetic saying often cited in Islamic thought)

In the end, truth does not belong to any sect, creed, or dogma. It belongs to those brave enough to seek it — within science, within scripture, and most of all, within themselves.

Final Reflection

This book began with a controversial phrase and has ended with a scientific defense of its meaning. Hallaj's *Ana al-Haqq* is not a declaration of personal divinity but a realization of divine truth flowing through the self once ego dissolves. In today's world, where consciousness is increasingly seen as the foundational reality of the cosmos, Hallaj's insight may not be heresy at all — it may be ahead of its time.

Let us not crucify our visionaries again. Let us understand them.

Let us meet *Haqq* — not in fear or tradition — but in awareness.
Ana al-Haqq — I am of the Truth, and the Truth is within me.

Chapter 18: Corruption of Higher Consciousness by Lower Minds: A Psychological and Societal Analysis

"They alter the words from their proper places..." — (Surah Al-Ma'idah 5:13)

The journey of human consciousness is neither linear nor uniformly distributed. It is a spectrum ranging from primal instincts to deeply evolved states of awareness. The tragedy of history, however, is that the most profound insights that arise from elevated states of consciousness are often misinterpreted, distorted, or even weaponized by individuals and groups operating from much lower states of mind. This chapter critically examines, through the lens of neuroscience, psychology, and Quranic logic, how higher consciousness is misused, misrepresented, and ultimately corrupted by lower minds.

1. Levels of Consciousness: The Neurophysiological Hierarchy

Consciousness, as neuroscience reveals, is not monolithic. It exists in various gradations, which correspond to different brainwave patterns—Delta (0.5–4 Hz), Theta (4–8 Hz), Alpha (8–13 Hz), Beta (13–30 Hz), and Gamma (30–100 Hz). Each of these states signifies different cognitive and experiential realities. Delta waves are associated with deep, dreamless sleep; Theta with subconscious and emotional states; Alpha with relaxed wakefulness; Beta with active problem-solving; and Gamma with heightened perception and unity of thought.

Individuals operating at higher frequencies, especially in Gamma wave states, often report experiences of deep interconnectedness, egoless awareness, profound empathy, and a sense of oneness with the cosmos. These states are biologically real and are documented in practitioners of deep meditation, contemplative traditions, and individuals reporting mystical experiences—without the need to invoke supernaturalism.

In such states, a person may come into contact with what the Quran calls **Al-Haqq**—the Ultimate Reality or Truth. In this elevated awareness, boundaries between the self and the cosmos dissolve. This is the realm from which statements like *Ana al-Haqq* emerge. It is not an egoistic claim but a dissolution of ego; not a declaration of divinity, but a realization of the interconnected essence of all things.

2. Lower Consciousness Reactions: Fear, Ego, and Misuse

However, when individuals with lower levels of consciousness encounter such ideas, their cognitive and emotional frameworks are often too narrow to comprehend them. The lower mind reacts not with openness, but with fear, resistance, or exploitation.

Fear stems from unfamiliarity. The ego feels threatened by truths that dissolve the illusion of separateness. This leads to aggression, mockery, or persecution—as was the case with Hallaj. Others, driven by jealousy or a craving for recognition, may not oppose the idea directly but seek to hijack it for personal or political gain.

In both cases, the essence of the message is lost. What remains is a hollow symbol—often branded, marketed, or turned into a cult.

3. Intentional Misinterpretation: From Ana al-Haqq to Marketable Myths

The history of spiritual and philosophical traditions is replete with examples where profound insights were turned into ritualistic dogmas. The statement *Ana al-Haqq*, originally a state of ego-death and divine alignment, was transformed into a mystical metaphor, adorned with stories of miracles, divine visions, and supernatural feats.

Such reinterpretation serves several motives:

- To gain followers who are awed by the spectacle rather than the substance
- To initiate new sects or religious traditions based on misunderstood ideas
- To accumulate social capital, wealth, or political influence

This is not merely a misreading—it is intellectual corruption. It is a betrayal of the original insight, much like forging a signature on a divine message for personal profit.

4. Group Psychology: How Societies Diminish Higher Ideas

Mass societies often function on cognitive simplicity. Complex, nuanced, or abstract ideas are typically rejected or repackaged into digestible narratives. In doing so, societies transform depth into shallowness.

A deep metaphysical statement becomes a slogan. A state of consciousness becomes a ritual. The person who uttered a truth becomes a 'saint' or a 'guru' with a marketable image. This societal mechanism flattens profound truths into consumable content. In a society dominated by low-conscious minds, the public spectacle replaces personal introspection.

Social media, religious branding, spiritual merchandise, and cults of personality all thrive in this climate. The original message—self-annihilation into truth—turns into its opposite: self-promotion through performance.

5. Quranic Warning Against This Behavior

The Quran explicitly warns against the alteration, concealment, and commodification of truth:

> *"They distort words from their [proper] usages..."* (Surah Al-Ma'idah 5:13)

> *"Woe to those who write the book with their own hands then say, 'This is from Allah'..."* (Surah Al-Baqarah 2:79)

These verses are not just about written scripture. They apply to all forms of altering, diluting, or exploiting truth for personal or group benefit. The Quran treats truth as sacred—and altering it as a grave moral and intellectual violation.

Ana al-Haqq is not blasphemy. Misrepresenting it is. The real sin is not to experience unity with Haqq, but to reduce it to superstition, profit, or prestige.

6. Neuroscience of Manipulation: Reward Over Truth

Low-level consciousness tends to operate primarily on the dopamine reward system. In such minds, the primary motivation is not truth or understanding, but gratification, social validation, and status.

This creates an inherent conflict: while the high-conscious mind seeks truth even at the cost of ego, the low-conscious mind seeks reward even at the cost of truth.

People in such states will reinterpret, reframe, or remix high-level ideas to fit their own cognitive frameworks. They will cherry-pick, oversimplify, or mythologize in order to make the idea more 'marketable'—be it in religious, political, or commercial arenas.

In such processes, the authenticity of the idea is sacrificed at the altar of social currency. The brain's default mode network (DMN), associated with narrative construction and ego-maintenance, becomes overactive, crafting stories and identities around these altered messages.

7. Historical Examples: Prophets and Their Hijacked Legacies

History offers numerous examples of how reformers, prophets, and mystics had their messages distorted after their deaths:

- Jesus, a radical ethical teacher, was transformed into a divine figure whose message was used to establish religious empires.
- Prophet Muhammad's Quranic vision of justice and personal accountability was fragmented into sects, schools, and political dynasties.
- Buddha's message of self-realization was turned into ritualistic traditions across various countries.
- Hallaj's non-dual realization became the cornerstone of mystical poetry, while his core insight was often buried under legends.

This distortion is not random—it is systematic. The human psyche, especially in its lower states, has a tendency to idolize what it cannot understand and to institutionalize what it cannot embody.

8. Conclusion: Preserving the Flame of Higher Consciousness

The *Ana al-Haqq* experience is a peak of human cognitive evolution. It is the point where the self recognizes its illusory separation and melts into the continuity of existence. It is a truth that must be lived, not sold; honored, not packaged.

Only a purified self (Nafs) and an awakened perceptive center (Qalb) can understand and preserve this experience. It requires a shift from egocentricity to egolessness, from belief to being, from reaction to reflection.

The Quran calls this state *Nafs al-Mutmainnah*—a self at peace with the Truth. And such a self does not seek followers or fame. It seeks alignment.

Let us end with a reminder:

> *"Do not follow what you have no knowledge of. Indeed, the hearing, the sight, and the heart—about all those [one] will be questioned."* (Surah Al-Isra 17:36)

The journey to Haqq is not external. It is inward. And only those who have transcended the noise of the ego can carry the silence of truth without distortion.

End Message

Truth is not a destination—it is a revelation within. Mansoor Al-Hallaj uttered "Ana al-Haqq" not to claim divinity, but to dissolve the illusion of separation between the self and the Source. His words were not arrogance; they were the final echo of unity realized.

This book has not aimed to explain God. It has aimed to liberate the reader from rigid structures that confine the self from knowing its own boundless nature. Through science, scripture, and consciousness, we have only scratched the surface of a reality far deeper than words can hold.

If this journey has stirred discomfort, it is a sign of growth. If it has evoked questions, it means you are alive to truth. And if it has offered even a glimpse of clarity, then it has fulfilled its purpose.

Remember—truth is not owned, inherited, or preached. It is realized. It burns silently within those who dare to question with sincerity and live with authenticity.

The path is not outward. It is inward.

The distance is not far. It is only veiled.

And the Divine is not separate. It is ***you****, when the self becomes still.*

Ana al-Haqq.

You are the Truth when you awaken.

— ***Harsa Khan***

Don't miss out!

Visit the website below and you can sign up to receive emails whenever Harsa khan publishes a new book. There's no charge and no obligation.

https://books2read.com/r/B-A-WBVVD-RGBJG

BOOKS 2 READ

Connecting independent readers to independent writers.

Did you love *Ana al-Haqq: Consciousness, Self, and the Quran, A SCIENTIFIC INTERPRETATION OF MANSOOR AL HALLAJ*? Then you should read *Decoding Masr: Quran, Civilization and Historical Distortion*[1] by Harsa khan!

[2]

What if Masr in the Qur'an was never Egypt?

What if centuries of tafsir were shaped not by divine clarity—but by imperial agendas?

In Decoding Masr, researcher and thinker Harsa Khan deconstructs one of the most deeply entrenched assumptions in Islamic exegesis—the equation of Qur'anic "Masr" with modern-day Egypt. Through linguistic forensics, archaeological comparisons, and civilizational analysis, this groundbreaking work challenges mainstream narratives inherited from Abbasid power centers and Western Orientalist thought.

Drawing from 16 rigorous chapters, the book explores the symbolic architecture of "Fir'aun," "Haman," and "Qarun" not as individuals, but as

1. https://books2read.com/u/bMda7a

2. https://books2read.com/u/bMda7a

systemic archetypes of tyranny, economic control, and scientific abuse. It questions why Qur'anic Masr resembles Harappan urban planning more than Nile civilization, and how clay brick towers echo in forgotten landscapes beyond Egypt.

This is not merely a historical correction—it is an intellectual rebellion. A manifesto against dogma and distortion, calling scholars, seekers, and reformers to re-read revelation through the lens of logic, science, and uncolonized thought.

Also by Harsa khan

Bani Israel: Ideology, Not Inheritance
Decoding Masr: Quran, Civilization and Historical Distortion
The Conscious Evolution: Reinterpreting Adam Through Science and Revelation
From Enlightenment to Empire: The Fall of Islam's Golden Age
Ana al-Haqq: Consciousness, Self, and the Quran, A SCIENTIFIC INTERPRETATION OF MANSOOR AL HALLAJ

Printed at Repro India Ltd.